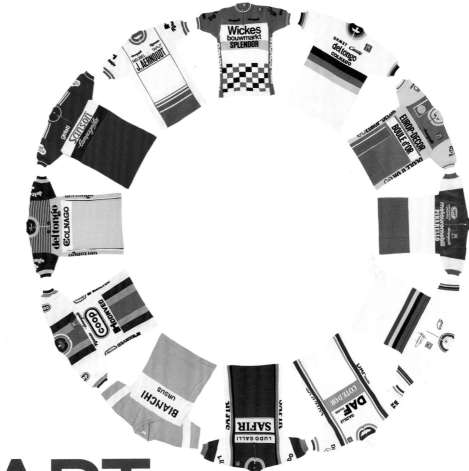

THE ART
OF THE JERSEY

ANDY STOREY

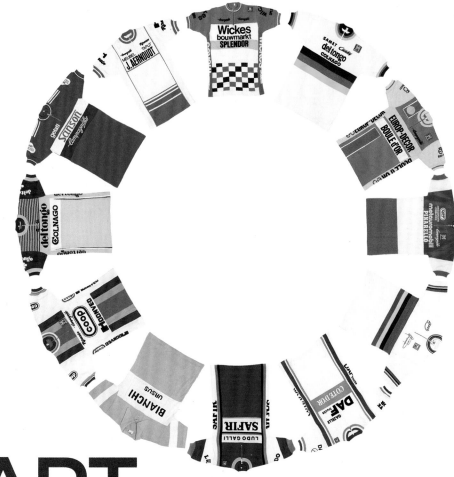

THE ART
OF THE JERSEY
A CELEBRATION OF THE CYCLING RACING JERSEY

MITCHELL BEAZLEY

CONTENTS

◄ Olympic champion Samuel Sánchez (Euskaltel) raises his hands in delight having won the 12th stage of the 2011 Tour de France. Sánchez wears a one-off team jersey by MOA.

INTRODUCTION

||||||||||||||||||||||||||||||||||||||||||||||||||||||||||||||||||||||||||||||||||||||||||

I find the design of cycle clothing a fascinating subject. Although I now work in the bicycle trade at Prendas Ciclismo, my love of cycling has been with me for far longer.

I was always riding my bicycle as a kid, and got my first serious bike (a Westlake MTB fitted with a Shimano Exage groupset) while still at school in 1987. This was when mountain biking was first catching on, its popularity due in part to a number of local windsurfing shops which stocked the bikes as alternative entertainment for when the wind was poor. I started riding a lot, and even entered the odd local race. A teacher encouraged me to ride in a "ten" organized by local club the Bournemouth Jubilee Wheelers, and I enjoyed the race so much I joined the club.

I wasn't in it alone, though. My younger brother also got himself a mountain bike and started his journey from being "Andy's brother" to a full-time cyclist and medallist at both the Beijing 2008 and

◀ Ireland's Sean Kelly (KAS) on the way to his second victory in the 1986 Paris–Roubaix. The KAS jersey that he wears is synonymous with his successes in professional racing.

London 2012 Paralympic Games. My dad also got fed up with just watching us race and started to get interested too.

The Bournemouth Jubilee Wheelers was where I also met my long-term friend and now employer Mick Tarrant. I first met Mick at Poole Track League where he would watch with his friends while I'd be racing a Rossin track bike around the cricket oval.

Over the years I built up a decent collection of cycle jerseys, many of which were purchased from Mick at a fledgling Prendas Ciclismo, which he was running out of his spare bedroom until the business was big enough to justify a commercial property and extra staff.

This book actually started life as a website, which I still run today. It took a year of work before the site was attracting a decent number of visitors, which currently stands at around 4,000 visits per month. I know that I am interested in the subject, but I'm always amazed where some of the text and photographs from the site end up, being used by specialist forums all the way up to articles on the *Telegraph* and *Guardian* sites, linking to my collection of jerseys.

So much has changed in the manufacture of cycling garments over the years and I hope to illustrate both old and new techniques, and showcase some stand-out designs that have become iconic, as well as some that are not so grand. I'll let you decide which ones are which!

▶ Wearing the Italian Tricolore in the 1976 Paris–Roubaix, Francesco Moser (Sanson) leads while Jan Raas (TI-Raleigh) struggles to hold his wheel. Neither man would win; that honour went to Marc Demeyer (Flandria-Velda) of Belgium.

THE EARLY YEARS

||||||||||||||||||||||||||||||||||||||||||||||||||||||||||||||||||||||||||||||||||||

Until the mid-seventies, cycling clothing had changed very little since the golden years of racing, when Coppi and Bartali battled it out both on and off the bike. The blend of choice was 50 per cent wool and 50 per cent acrylic for both the jersey and the bib shorts, with the seat pad made from Chamois deer hides (which is why some people still refer to a seat pad as a "chamois").

Textiles came in solid colours, so it was still genuinely time consuming and difficult to make cycle jerseys with elaborate patterns and designs. Sponsor names and logos were embroidered directly on to the garments by skilled workers and the collars of many jerseys still featured button closures, although zips soon came along.

As an increasing number of sponsors' names were added to both jerseys and shorts, embroidered logos were often replaced by cloth badges and patches, and a new process called flocking was developed. The process involved applying small fibre particles to the surface of the garment and bonding them in place with a special hot adhesive applied in the shape of the logo or text. Flocking produced a smooth and neat finish, but it did tend to lift off after repeated washing and general wear.

Both Castelli and Assos claim to have introduced Lycra cycling shorts to the professional peloton. They were initially met with scepticism, but when top teams like TI-Raleigh took them on, everyone wanted them!

◀ Gino Bartali (left), Alfredo Binda (second left) and Fausto Coppi (right) were giants of the sport in the fifties, when technical sport clothing was in its infancy. Their woollen jerseys then featured wing collars, which were buttoned down at the back, as well as chest and rear pockets.

BIANCHI/URSUS REPLICA TEAM WOOL JERSEY

Manufacturer: Santini

Associated bike: Bianchi

Key rider: Fausto Coppi

This jersey is a tribute to the golden age of cycling style. It was made as a prop for the 1995 film *Il Grande Fausto*, which tells the story of Fausto Coppi. Sergio Castellitto played Coppi in the film, wearing this fabulous jersey made from 80 per cent wool and 20 per cent acrylic, with fold-down collar and buttons at the neck. The period feel was continued with buttoned pockets on the front and back of the jersey, and the exact hue of blue that Bianchi used in the fifties. Over the years, the colour of Bianchi bikes has gone from this blue shade to a greener hue. Nice as the modern green is, there's something special about the original blue.

This was not the only jersey that Santini made for the film (see opposite).

1952

LEGNANO/ PIRELLI REPLICA TEAM WOOL JERSEY

Manufacturer: Santini
Associated bike: Legnano
Key rider: Gino Bartali

Another replica jersey produced by Santini for *Il Grande Fausto* (see opposite), this iconic green and red design is most famous for being worn by the great Gino Bartali, winner of the 1948 Tour de France.

The embroidered lettering on the front and sleeves of the jersey is beautiful, and the pearl buttons on the collar and pockets are a simple yet classic touch.

1952

ATALA/PIRELLI REPLICA TEAM WOOL JERSEY

Manufacturer: Santini
Associated bike: Atala
Key rider: Fausto Coppi

This replica jersey was also produced for *Il Grande Fausto* (see opposite). Fausto Coppi won the Giro d'Italia five times and the Tour de France twice, and was the first rider in history to win both in the same year. That year was 1952, the year he wore this classic, chic jersey.

This double was later matched by Jacques Anquetil in 1964, Stephen Roche in 1987, and Marco Pantani in 1998. Bernard Hinault and Miguel Indurain each achieved this feat twice, but Eddy Merckx tops the list with three doubles, in 1970, 1972, and 1974.

1970
BIC TEAM WOOL JERSEY

Manufacturer: Unknown
Associated bike: Motobécane
Key rider: Luis Ocaña

This punchy design was worn by Luis Ocaña's team in the seventies, but due to its construction, I believe this particular example was made for a semi-pro Belgian team that was active in the same period.

BIC Boy, the company's trusty mascot, is instantly recognizable, as is the BIC logo. Both were added to this jersey as heat-applied felt.

While the BIC team have long disappeared from the professional peloton, the company re-emerged in 2015 to sponsor the Vuelta a España, bringing the once-familiar logo back to the pro cycling scene.

1970

SCIC CUCINE COMPONIBILI TEAM WOOL JERSEY

Manufacturer: Santini
Associated bike: Colnago
Key rider: Giuseppe Saronni

This simple yet bold monochrome design was in the professional peloton for ten years, with SCIC (an Italian kitchen company) the headline sponsor for the team.

The company presumably decided to increase brand awareness in their home market, so by sponsoring a team that featured some of the greatest Italian cyclists of the era – Giuseppe Saronni, Vittorio Adorni, and Gianbattista Baronchelli – the plan was bound to work!

This original team-issue jersey was produced by Santini. However, competing manufacturer De Marchi recently produced an accurate replica in Merino wool.

1972
MOLTENI ARCORE REPLICA TEAM JERSEY

Manufacturer: Santini
Associated bike: Eddy Merckx
Key rider: Eddy Merckx

Open a book about Eddy Merckx and you are likely to see a picture of the best male cyclist of all time wearing a Molteni Arcore jersey. This is a replica of that iconic design, and despite his time in various other teams and jerseys, including GS Solo/Superia, Peugeot, Faema, Fiat, and C&A, the Molteni jersey is the one everyone remembers him in.

The team also boasted Gianni Motta and Marino Basso, who contributed over 80 wins between them, but it was Merckx who provided the majority of the team's 600 victories.

In case you were wondering who the headline sponsor was, Molteni was a sausage manufacturer based in the town of Arcore, near Milan.

1973
BIANCHI/ CAMPAGNOLO REPLICA TEAM WOOL JERSEY

Manufacturer: Santini

Associated bike: Bianchi

Key rider: Felice Gimondi

Designed for the riders in the 2012 Granfondo Felice Gimondi, this wool/acrylic mix replica jersey is based on the 1973–6 Bianchi/ Campagnolo pro team jersey. It features the rainbow bands on the sleeves and collar, just like Gimondi wore back in the day.

The two logos on the front and shoulders are embroidered, as they would have been when the jersey was first made, in the days before man-made fibres and modern printing techniques. The only concession to modernity on this replica jersey is the 14cm (5½ inch) zip at the neck.

17

REPLICA ITALIAN NATIONAL JERSEY WITH BIANCHI/ CAMPAGNOLO

Manufacturer: Santini

Associated bike: Bianchi

Key rider: Felice Gimondi

This beautiful, vivid *azzurro* blue jersey was available to the riders in the 2014 Granfondo Felice Gimondi. It is a replica of the jersey that Gimondi wore during his victory at the 1973 World Championships in Barcelona, riding a Bianchi bike with Campagnolo components.

All of the jersey's logos and badges are embroidered to give it an authentic retro look, but it is made from a practical 50 per cent wool and 50 per cent acrylic mix to make it easier to care for. Gimondi's signature adorns the chest of the jersey, giving a nice touch.

1973

REPLICA ITALIAN NATIONAL JERSEY WITH BIANCHI/ CAMPAGNOLO

Manufacturer: Santini

Associated bike: Bianchi

Key rider: Felice Gimondi

This classic-looking jersey is a modern replica created to celebrate Felice Gimondi's life-long association with Bianchi. It was made available to the riders who took part in the 2011 Granfondo Felice Gimondi, an annual cycling event held in Bergamo, Italy.

Felice Gimondi was crowned the champion of Italy in 1972. Based in Bergamo, in the same town as Santini, Gimondi still plays a very active role at Bianchi and continues to be a great ambassador for the company. This wool jersey is not only a classic design, but is also beautifully hand made by Santini.

1975

FLANDRIA/ CARPENTER/ CONFORTLUXE/ PUMA TEAM WOOL JERSEY

Manufacturer: Tricodnar

Associated bike: Flandria

Key riders: Freddy Maertens, Walter Godefroot

This is a rare original pro team jersey, made for either Freddy Maertens or Walter Godefroot while riding for the mighty Flandria team. The team was a huge presence in the peloton in the mid-seventies.

Aside from the switching of minor sponsors, the jersey's striking styling did not change that much over the years; the red colour and bold black lettering were a constant.

Although Puma was the headline sponsor, the jersey was made by Belgian manufacturer Tricodnar, who also made the stunning Safir/ Geuze team jersey on page 23.

TI-RALEIGH/ CAMPAGNOLO TEAM WOOL JERSEY

Manufacturer: Santini

Associated bike: Raleigh

Key rider: none

My first proper bike was a Raleigh – a Grifter, to be precise – and I'm sure I'm not alone. Long before cycling was popular in the UK, Raleigh was a household name and it's not a stretch of the imagination to assume that their sponsorship of the TI-Raleigh team was an attempt to break into the European market.

Alongside the Molteni Arcore jersey (see page 16), the design of this wool jersey is among the most instantly recognizable in the history of cycling, with its brash blend of bright red and yellow, and its harsh black sleeves. This is a true classic.

▶ As befits a former World Champion, Jan Raas (TI-Raleigh) is shown here wearing the rainbow bands of victory on the collar of his team jersey, reminding us of his achievement.

1977

BROOKLYN CHEWING GUM TEAM WOOL JERSEY

Manufacturer: Santini
Associated bike: GIOS
Key rider: Roger De Vlaeminck

Roger De Vlaeminck rode 14 editions of the Paris–Roubaix race, winning it on 4 occasions, without suffering a single puncture thanks to his remarkable skill over the unforgiving cobbles of the route. De Vlaeminck won the 1977 Tour of Flanders, the Milan–San Remo three times, as well as the World Cyclo-cross Championships in 1975.

This original wool jersey, worn by De Vlaeminck while he rode for the Brooklyn Chewing Gum team, is a beautiful design, especially considering that jersey printing techniques were not to come along for another 15 years. The stripes were achieved by stitching together wool/acrylic mix panels. The sponsor panel is made from white fabric, stitched on to the jersey with the sponsor's lettering embroidered in black.

1979

SAFIR/GEUZE/ ST LOUIS/LUDO/ TRICODNAR TEAM WOOL JERSEY

Manufacturer: Tricodnar
Associated bike: Ludo
Key rider: Benny Schepmans

This rare, original pro team jersey was made at the end of the seventies by the French manufacturer Tricodnar, who are now sadly no longer in business.

While the flock lettering makes a bold statement, it's the level of detail elsewhere in this woollen garment that makes the design so special, particularly the bright bands of colour.

After producing a yellow and blue striped jersey for the team the previous year, rather reminiscent of the Brooklyn jersey opposite, Tricodnar used a number of different panels to help this jersey stand out in the peloton.

THE
EIGHTIES

||||||||||||||||||||||||||||||||||||||||||||||||||||||||||||||||||||||||||||||||||||||||||||||||||||||||

Without doubt, the eighties witnessed the greatest changes in the production of cycle clothing. At the beginning of the decade, wool garments ruled the professional peloton (there are some fine examples coming up in this chapter) but by the end polyester was everywhere.

In 1981, Castelli outfitted a handful of riders with turquoise Lycra shorts for the Giro d'Italia, at a time when only black shorts were allowed. The riders came to the start line in woollen leggings, then revealed their shorts as the race began. Race officials fined Castelli for the stunt, but the media frenzy made it all worthwhile.

By the mid-eighties, many manufacturers were starting to adopt a new technology of dye-sublimation printing, which allowed graphics and sponsor names to be printed directly on to white polyester. A mirror image of the design is made on heat-resistant transfer paper and applied to the fabric using heat and pressure.

This process improved flexibility and greatly reduced the cost of production, giving the jersey designers and sponsors a freer rein to create the designs of their choice.

Ironically, after years of investment in sublimation machinery, some manufacturers are re-investing in machinery capable of producing wool garments. Such is the popularity of retro, thanks in part to events like L'Eroica, there is now a genuine demand for wool cycling jerseys. Many manufacturers simply outsource the work, but some artisans prefer to produce in house.

◀ Gilbert Duclos-Lassalle leads former winner Francesco Moser in the 1983 edition of the Paris–Roubaix, but it was the Dutchman Andreas "Hennie" Kuiper (Aernoudt Rossin) who went on to win. Duclos-Lassalle would have to wait a further ten years before he won the race.

1980

CILO/AUFINA TEAM WOOL JERSEY

Manufacturer: Santini

Associated bike: Cilo

Key rider: Beat Breu

The minimalist and classy design of this wool jersey is instantly recognizable and always admired.

Today's peloton is awash with the concept of "marginal gains", but in 1980 Beat Breu was unusual in his embrace of the idea. The Swiss climber believed that saving weight on his bike was paramount, even removing his handlebar tape to gain precious seconds.

Breu enjoyed a very successful stint in cyclo-cross at the end of his career; he was twice National Champion and finished third at the World Championships in 1988.

Cilo was also behind the shocking pink and yellow kit and bike frames of the Cilo mountain bike team during the early days of mountain biking. Fans needed sunglasses to watch them compete in the cross country and downhill rounds of the Grundig World Cup Series.

1980

LA REDOUTE/ MOTOBÉCANE/ TRICODNAR TEAM WOOL JERSEY

Manufacturer: Tricodnar

Associated bike: Motobécane

Key riders: Paul Sherwen, Jean-François Pescheux

Although 1980 saw the La Redoute team win two stages of the Tour de France and two stages in Paris–Nice, some of the riders from that year went on to greater success when they retired from the peloton.

Jean-François Pescheux became a technical director at Amaury Sport Organization (ASO), the organizers of the Tour de France and the Vuelta a España, while Paul Sherwen is well known for his work with Phil Liggett, bringing commentary to many professional bike races.

This delightful design, with its bold chevrons, is a personal favourite.

1980

GS SPORTMAN/ CABLE/CASTELLI TEAM WOOL JERSEY

Manufacturer: Castelli

Associated bike: none

Key rider: none

The origins of this jersey are obscure, but it's undoubtedly a beautiful design and one that oozes class. And, of course, it has the all-important Castelli logo on the shoulder.

The iconic Castelli scorpion first appeared in 1974 and was designed by Maurizio Castelli himself. Although it has evolved over time, put the logo in front of any racing cyclist and they'll immediately tell you what the brand is.

GELATI SANSON/ CAMPAGNOLO TEAM WOOL JERSEY

Manufacturer: *Santini*

Associated bike: F Moser

Key rider: Francesco Moser

Many of the fans who are new to cycling will not be familiar with the imposing figure of Francesco Moser thundering across the cobbles on his way to victory in the Paris–Roubaix, wearing this iconic Sanson jersey.

This jersey is a great example of how a very simple, yet striking design can stand the test of time. The deep green colour of the jersey no doubt influenced Sir Paul Smith when he designed the "Grand Départ" celebration jersey for the 2007 Tour de France, which started in London.

1981
COTE D'OR/ DAF TRUCKS/ GAZELLE/ SANTINI TEAM WOOL JERSEY

Manufacturer: Santini

Associated bike: Gazelle

Key rider: Roger De Vlaeminck

Most fans will remember Roger De Vlaeminck wearing the iconic Brooklyn jersey (see page 22), but he also rode for Côte d'Or/DAF Trucks/Gazelle during the 1981 and 1982 seasons, winning the Belgian National Championships and Paris–Brussels, and finishing second in Milan–San Remo, Paris–Roubaix, and Amstel Gold.

The sponsor names on this jersey are made with flock lettering, while the wool knit adds colour. The sponsor panel on the back of the jersey follows the style of the front, while further details include a simple three-colour collar and sleeve cuffs, and an early Santini-branded zip finishing off the garment.

1981
SAFIR/LUDO/
GALLI TEAM
WOOL JERSEY

Manufacturer: Santini

Associated bike: Ludo

Key rider: Herman Van Springel

The Safir/Ludo/Galli team worked around the fabulously named Herman Van Springel, who spent his final year as a pro with the team and won the incredibly lengthy Bordeaux–Paris pro race for the seventh time.

Most of the team's 20 riders were Belgian, but early Australian pioneer John Trevorrow was there, as well as Canadians Richard Meehan and Ron Hayman (latterly of the US 7-Eleven team).

The back of this jersey is virtually identical to the front and it is interesting to note that it only has two buttoned pockets. The very neat Santini embroidered badge still looks good today.

SANTINI/SELLE ITALIA TEAM WOOL JERSEY

Manufacturer: Santini

Associated bike: none

Key rider: none

You might think that Santini Maglificio Sportivo, the clothing company that made this jersey, were the title sponsor of this team – but they weren't. According to Pietro Santini, the title sponsor was, coincidentally, "another Santini", also from Bergamo.

Pietro Santini has seen his company grow from its humble beginnings in 1965, selling wool jerseys locally, to a truly international company producing over 3,000 items a day in Italy, and exporting three-quarters of its output around the world.

This businesslike design makes great use of just three colours and combines tall and slender fonts to represent the two sponsors.

1982
DEL TONGO/ COLNAGO/ CAMPAGNOLO TEAM WOOL JERSEY

Manufacturer: Castelli

Associated bike: Colnago

Key rider: Giuseppe Saronni

This is an iconic jersey design. The Del Tongo/Colnago team were clothed by a number of different garment manufacturers over the years, including Castelli, Parentini and, finally, Santini.

The team had some great champions on the road. In 1982 Giuseppe Saronni won the World Road Championship at Goodwood Motor Racing Circuit, beating Greg LeMond. He followed that success with a victory in the Giro di Lombardia, wearing the rainbow-striped jersey.

1982
GIS GELATI/ OLMO/ CAMPAGNOLO TEAM WOOL JERSEY

Manufacturer: Santini

Associated bike: Olmo Bikes

Key riders: Eddy Schepers, Simone Fraccaro

This stunning navy blue team training jersey is from the 1982 season and would have been worn by the team riders before and after their races. Essentially, unless conditions were extremely cold, riders would have only worn a long-sleeved jersey in training, and pre- and post-competition.

The team would also have worn this long-sleeved jersey during training, as truly thermal garments would not appear in the peloton until the mid-eighties.

After his riding career, Simone Fraccaro set up clothing company Giessegi (GSG) and became manager of the Pepsi/Fanini team.

1982
SPLENDOR/ WICKES BOUWMARKT/ CAMPAGNOLO TEAM WOOL JERSEY

Manufacturer: Santini

Associated bike: Splendor

Key rider: Claude Criquielion

It is not until you see the reverse side of the chequerboard panel on this jersey that you truly appreciate the lengths manufacturers like Santini had to go to before the days of sublimation (printing designs on to high-performance fabrics).

Each strip of squares was produced separately, then they were stitched together to create the chequerboard effect, allowing Claude Criquielion and his team mates to stand out in the peloton.

In the days before sublimation, a huge amount of work was required to produce all of the sponsor logos. This jersey features a combination of flock and embroidered logos.

1983

J AERNOUDT MEUBELEN/ ROSSIN/ CAMPAGNOLO TEAM WOOL JERSEY

Manufacturer: Santini
Associated bike: Rossin
Key rider: Hennie Kuiper

Hennie Kuiper wore this simple, no-nonsense jersey design during his victory at the 1983 Paris–Roubaix. Kuiper won a huge variety of races during his career; he won stages at the Grand Tours, was an Olympic and World Champion, and re-invented himself later on, winning the Paris–Roubaix on his 11th attempt.

Kuiper raced for many different teams, including TI-Raleigh, Peugeot, DAF Trucks, Kwantum Hallen, Skala/Roland, and Sigma; examples of the jerseys that were worn by all the teams can be found throughout this book.

▶ Dutchman Hennie Kuiper (Aernoudt Rossin) took his one and only win at Roubaix wearing an Italian wool jersey made by Santini for a Belgian team.

1983
REYNOLDS ALUMINIO/GALLI/ CAMPAGNOLO TEAM JERSEY

Manufacturer: Etxeondo
....
Associated bike: Pinarello
....
Key rider: Pedro Delgado

This Reynolds jersey is from the 1983 season, which can be considered the point at which the popularity of modern polyester jerseys outstripped that of old-style woollen jerseys.

The shape and cut of this jersey looks slightly odd now, but manufacturer Etxeondo was ahead of many of its competitors in its adoption of modern fabrics, as it still is today.

If you are a traditionalist, however, don't despair: the woollen jersey continued to play a part in the peloton for some years to come.

1983

METAURO MOBILI/ PINARELLO TEAM WOOL JERSEY

Manufacturer: Santini

Associated bike: Pinarello

Key rider: Flavio Zappi

This dramatic, well-structured 1983 version of the Metauro Mobili/Pinarello team jersey features more blue than the following year's jersey (see page 45).

Although Flavio Zappi was not the biggest name in the team – that was really Lucien Van Impe – many young British hopefuls have Flavio to thank for the start of their professional careers as he now runs a successful feeder team that helps promising riders into the European peloton.

1983

BELGIAN NATIONAL CHAMPION WOOL JERSEY WITH METAURO MOBILI/ PINARELLO

Manufacturer: Santini

Associated bike: Pinarello

Key rider: Lucien Van Impe

Lucien Van Impe won the Tour de France King of the Mountains title in 1983, just weeks after winning his National Championships in Belgium.

With the highly changeable conditions in the mountains during the Tour in July, where temperatures can vary by as much as 30°C (86°F) during a single stage, it makes you wonder how much the old woollen jerseys, such as this conservative Belgian National Champion design, hampered the riders' performances, compared with the technical garments they have today – not to mention the old steel bikes which were heavier than modern bikes.

RENAULT/ELF/ CYCLES GITANE TEAM JERSEY

Manufacturer: Castelli

Associated bike: Cycles Gitane

Key riders: Bernard Hinault, Greg LeMond

The powerful Renault/Elf team was in action from 1978 until 1985, with wins throughout the seasons, mainly due to the calibre of team leader Bernard Hinault.

This team jersey, made by Castelli, was and still is a striking design. Castelli was an early pioneer of the sublimation process which finally allowed graphics and logos to be printed directly on to fabric. An additional innovation by Castelli enabled Hinault to wear a windproof jersey for his victory in the 1983 edition of the Flèche Wallonne.

It is interesting to note that the Castelli logo on this jersey is printed as part of the production process and is not reproduced in the more common red and white colours.

1984
CAMPAGNOLO WOOL JERSEY

Manufacturer: *Santini*

Associated bike: none

Key rider: none

During the 1980s, Campagnolo had far less competition for their groupsets (the mechanical parts of a bike). Now their products have to compete with those of Shimano, FSA, and SRAM in a highly competitive market. However, the Campagnolo name still carries a tremendous amount of prestige and, as it did in the eighties, their name sells products.

Unfortunately Campagnolo no longer have their own brand of cycle clothing, like this jersey, as they discontinued the line in 2012. Fans of this long-standing brand now have to find other ways of showing their affection.

The design of this simple yet bold jersey primarily revolves around the classic Campagnolo lettering that is positioned across the chest.

1984
WORLD CHAMPION WOOL JERSEY WITH GS GUERCIOTTI

Manufacturer: Santini
Associated bike: Guerciotti
Key rider: Roland Liboton

Until recently I hadn't been able to uncover the history of this jersey. However, some detailed research revealed that it was almost certainly made for Roland Liboton for a Guerciotti-branded team.

The super-bold Guerciotti star logo is a sewn-on badge, and white flock lettering has been applied to the chest of this 80 per cent wool-mix jersey. A good-quality YKK zip has been used for practicality, but it does unfortunately cut straight though those iconic rainbow bands at the neck and waist.

1984
MOTOBÉCANE TEAM WOOL JERSEY

Manufacturer: Santini
Associated bike: Motobécane
Key rider: none

This Motobécane jersey was not made for a professional cycling team, but was made to promote the French bicycle manufacturer. Motobécane's bold logo, using the colours of the French tricolore flag, is simple yet very effective.

Motobécane filed for bankruptcy and reformed in 1984 as MBK, using both the MBK and Motobécane logos that year. During the explosion in popularity of the mountain bike, MBK made some multi-coloured Day-Glo models and latterly sponsored the Cofidis team with some high-end road bikes. Unfortunately the company now only makes mopeds for the European market.

1984
PEUGEOT/ MICHELIN/SHELL TEAM WOOL JERSEY

Manufacturer: Santini
Associated bike: Cycles Peugeot
Key riders: Robert Millar, Sean Yates

Peugeot has a long history in the sponsorship of cycling teams, with various sub-sponsors coming and going during the team's history. The petroleum companies Shell, BP, and Esso, for example, were often present on the sleeves of riders like Millar and Yates.

While earlier team-issue jerseys would have used embroidery for the sponsor logos, this particular example uses flock lettering on the wool, which is not unusual for the period in which it was produced.

What is unusual, however, is the use of flock squares to create the chequerboard design. Santini also made later, polyester versions of this jersey, using sublimation to achieve the design.

1984
EUROP-DECOR/ BOULE D'OR/ EDDY MERCKX TEAM WOOL JERSEY

Manufacturer: Santini

Associated bike:
Eddy Merckx Cycles

Key rider: Frank Hoste

Despite Gerrie Knetemann's victory in the GP Pino Cerami, and Alfons De Wolf's win in Stage 14 of the Tour de France and Stage 1 of the Tour de Romandie, the highlight of this Belgian team's history has to be Frank Hoste taking three stages and the green points jersey in the 1984 Tour de France.

The jersey he wore combined various manufacturing techniques, including the use of multiple panels, flock lettering, and sewn-on badges. As a nice extra touch, there is also an Eddy Merckx fabric label on the inside of the jersey.

1984
ITALIAN NATIONAL CHAMPION WOOL JERSEY WITH METAURO MOBILI/ PINARELLO

Manufacturer: Santini
Associated bike: Pinarello
Key rider: Vittorio Algeri

This stunning wool jersey was hand made in Italy by Santini for 1984 Italian National Champion Vittorio Algeri. Both Santini and Algeri are from Bergamo, so it must have been nice for Santini to see a local lad win the national title.

This bold wool jersey features a combination of embroidery, sewn-on badges, and flock lettering to represent the sponsors. Santini used a green zip to keep the look of the jersey as clean as possible.

COOP/HOONVED/ ROSSIN/ CAMPAGNOLO TEAM WOOL JERSEY

Manufacturer: Santini

Associated bike: Rossin

Key rider: John Herety

Kim Andersen was the big winner for the Coop/Hoonved team in 1984, with victories in the Flèche Wallonne, Tour du Limousin, and the Tour de Vendée, but it was John Herety's name that surprised me in the list of team riders.

Herety is one of the UK's most prolific and well-liked cycling managers, who started off his management career while still riding with the Percy Bilton team in 1986.

Santini made the most of the improvements in manufacturing technology to make this striking jersey – each of the logos is flocked on to the jersey, saving valuable manufacturing time compared with embroidering them.

1984
METAURO MOBILI/ PINARELLO TEAM WOOL JERSEY

Manufacturer: Santini

Associated bike: Pinarello

Key riders: Lucien Van Impe, Johan van der Velde

The stripes on this jersey design, would have really stood out in the European peloton. The white chest panel found on this 1984 version, which didn't appear on the previous year's jersey (see page 37), breaks up the blue and yellow colours and makes the team's sponsors stand out with better effect, too.

Although 1984 was the better year for jersey design, it was not a good year for team leader Lucien Van Impe. He won the King of the Mountains competition in the Tour de France in 1983 but didn't win a single race in 1984!

1985
LA VIE CLAIRE/ RADAR/WONDER TEAM WOOL JERSEY

Manufacturer: Santini

Associated bike: Look Cycle

Key riders: Bernard Hinault, Greg LeMond

This stunning jersey design was inspired by the work of Dutch artist Piet Mondrian, and was singled out for praise in Bernard Hinault's autobiography, *Memories of the Peloton*. Hinault explains that the team wanted to stand out and brighten up the peloton. They first selected an all-black strip, but later discarded it due to the extreme heat of summer races like the Tour de France.

The jersey was created at the same time that the pro teams were swapping from wool/acrylic jerseys to modern polyesters. It was constructed using several different panels of wool, stitched together to provide the geometric pattern. Flock lettering was used for the sponsor logos, and an embroidered Santini badge for the brand logo.

▶ Bernard Hinault was instrumental in the decision to ditch an all-black jersey design for this iconic Mondrian-inspired jersey.

NIKON/VAN SCHILT/ELRO SNACKS/ COLNAGO TEAM WOOL JERSEY

Manufacturer: Decca
....
Associated bike: Colnago
....
Key rider: none

M any people will not have heard of this mid-eighties cycling team, but in 1988 it morphed into the TVM/Van Schilt team, made famous by riders such as Phil Anderson, Johan Capiot, Jesper Skibby, and Scott Sunderland.

Decca was an important presence in the cycle-clothing market in the eighties, but it would only be through their sponsorship of the Russian Katusha team in 2014 that many new cyclists would have seen their name in the headlines.

A full YKK zip cuts through the centre of this long-sleeved training jersey. The manufacturing techniques employed in its production would have made it difficult to marry up the lettering either side of the zip.

1985
GS DEL TONGO/ COLNAGO TEAM WOOL JERSEY

Manufacturer: Santini

Associated bike: Colnago

Key rider: none

This is not the design that is usually associated with the Del Tongo/Colnago team, so it's more likely that the jersey was made for an amateur feeder team. Even so, this original team jersey, made with a fairly typical mix of 80 per cent wool and 20 per cent acrylic, is also attractive. There are three buttoned rear pockets, and flock lettering has been used for the logos.

With the end of wool jersey production imminent, Santini would in 1985 have been investing heavily in new machinery to take on the trend for polyester-based jerseys in future years.

1985
BELGIAN NATIONAL TEAM WOOL JERSEY

Manufacturer: Santini

Associated bike: none

Key rider: none

I've always been amazed at how strong this jersey design is, despite its simplicity. The tri-colour band of the national flag is nicely framed by the blue hue of the jersey, the colour that is still in use today.

Interestingly, this jersey has no rear pockets so was probably used either on the track or for a podium presentation. This particular jersey has found a good home with a friend in Belgium, who wears it when he takes his retro Eddy Merckx steel bike out for a ride.

1985

KWANTUM HALLEN/ DECOSOL/YOKO/ COLNAGO TEAM JERSEY

Manufacturer: Decca

Associated bike: Colnago

Key rider: Jan Raas

A direct link can be found between this mid-eighties team and the LottoNL/Jumbo cycling team (see page 214), which was to be found in the peloton 30 years later.

The team was founded in 1984 under the name Kwantum, when the mighty TI-Raleigh team split after star rider Jan Raas and team leader Peter Post fell out. The lead sponsor was succeeded by SuperConfex, Buckler, WordPerfect, Novell, Rabobank, Blanco, and Belkin, with LottoNL/Jumbo taking over in 2015.

A huge amount of work went into making this jersey, which is constructed from numerous panels. This is no real surprise given that it was made for a professional rider, and not for commercial resale.

1985
GERMAN NATIONAL CHAMPION WOOL JERSEY WITH DEL TONGO/ COLNAGO

Manufacturer: Santini

Associated bike: Colnago

Key rider: Rolf Gölz

Although many will be familiar with its yellow and blue jersey design, less are aware that the Del Tongo team also had a number of World and National Champions among its riders, wearing jerseys to reflect their status.

World Champion Giuseppe Saronni is without question the best known, but his brother Antonio was Italian Cyclo-cross Champion, and Rolf Gölz was crowned German Road Race Champion in 1985.

For every year after his victory, Gölz would be able to display the German colours on the collar and cuffs of each team jersey he wore.

COSMETICI MALVOR/SIDI/ BOTTECCHIA/ VAPORELLA/ MODOLO TEAM JERSEY

Manufacturer: Assos

Associated bike: Bottecchia

Key rider: Acácio da Silva

There is no getting away from the fact that there are too many different logos and fonts on this, another classic eighties jersey made by Assos, making the design rather too busy. Modern printing techniques came with some disadvantages, namely cluttered jersey designs.

Acácio da Silva was the best performer for the team in 1985, with stage wins in the Giro d'Italia, Tour de Romandie, and the Prologue of the Tour de Suisse. The team's sponsors came and went during the eighties and it eventually morphed into the ZG Mobili/Selle Italia/ Bottecchia team (see page 74).

1986
KAS REPLICA TEAM JERSEY

Manufacturer: Etxeondo
Associated bike: Vitus Bikes
Key rider: Sean Kelly

Irishman Sean "King" Kelly turned professional in 1977, immediately making an impression on the peloton at a time when successful riders from countries outside of the European heartlands were rare.

Kelly is mostly associated with the KAS team, and this Etxeondo replica jersey is virtually identical to his team jersey of the time, the classic and minimal design of which still looks classy today. In his 18-year career as a professional, Kelly won numerous single-day classics and the 1988 Vuelta a España, as well as seven successive victories at Paris–Nice.

1987
ADR/FANGIO/ IOC/MBK TEAM JERSEY

Manufacturer: Fangio
Associated bike: MBK
Key rider: Dirk Demol

The best-remembered ADR jersey among cycling fans is the Tour de France-winning 1989 version (see page 62), the fluorescent yellow number Greg LeMond wore on his road to victory. Even so, this 1987 jersey is still a great-looking design.

Out of all of the riders on the 1987 roster, Dirk Demol had perhaps the greatest success, winning the 1988 edition of Paris–Roubaix and subsequently taking a job with Discovery/RadioShack/Trek Factory Racing as a Sports Director.

SKALA/ROLAND TEAM JERSEY

Manufacturer: unknown

Associated bike: Colnago

Key riders: Brian Holm, Jesper Skibby

The Skala/Roland team came into being, as they so often do, as a result of two teams merging – in this case Skala/Skil and Roland/Van de Ven. The Skala team can trace its roots back to the Europ-Decor/Boule d'Or team (see page 42), and the Roland team back to the Safir/Ludo/Galli team (see page 30).

I remember a fair few club riders wearing this jersey design at the end of the eighties, the big keyboard on the front making it stand out in a way unique to that decade. It is not always obvious what sponsors actually produce and are promoting to their customers, but Roland certainly made it clear for cycling fans.

REYNOLDS ALUMINIO/ ETXEONDO/ PINARELLO REPLICA TEAM JERSEY

Manufacturer: Etxeondo

Associated bike: Pinarello

Key rider: Pedro Delgado

I make no secret of my love for Etxeondo (pronounced "Etch-a-ondo") cycle clothing. I purchased this jersey in 2014, a replica of the kit Pedro Delgado wore to victory in the 1988 Tour de France. This jersey is made from modern fabrics, but it is an exact copy of the original design.

Delgado now organizes an annual sportif in Spain and he asked Etxeondo to make him a replica jersey for the occasion. With great attention to detail, they included the old version of the Etxeondo logo. As you can see, it used to be two words. The E and O make up the logo, which represents a traditional Basque haystack.

1988

SIGMA PAINTS/ FINA/FORD/CICLI DIAMANT TEAM JERSEY

Manufacturer: Santini

Associated bike: Cicli Diamant

Key rider: Hennie Kuiper

What better way is there for a Belgian paint manufacturer to advertise than on a colourful pro cycling team jersey?

Sometimes sponsors do not need to promote their brand and prove to the board the worthwhile return on their investment. It is often simply that the business owner is in love with cycling. However, in this example, the sponsorship would no doubt have been a success as cycling is so popular in Belgium.

1988

PEPSI/FANINI/ GSG TEAM JERSEY

Manufacturer: Giessegi

Associated bike: Alan

Key rider: Stefano Tomasini

Despite a thoroughly American lead sponsor, the Pepsi/ Fanini team had their heart in Italy. Managed by GSG's Simone Fraccaro, they took part in the Giro d'Italia, with Stefano Tomasini taking the young rider's classification.

This is a fairly typical bold design from the period, with the Pepsi logo taking centre stage and the stars on the side panels hinting at the American sponsor's flag.

1988
CERAMICHE ARIOSTEA TEAM JERSEY

Manufacturer: Vittore Gianni

Associated bike: De Rosa

Key rider: Rolf Sørensen

Ariostea was an Italian professional cycling team from 1984 to 1993. The infamous Giancarlo Ferretti was the Sports Director, leading the team to achieve greater prominence in the peloton.

Vittore Gianni may not be a familiar name today, but the manufacturer Castelli traces its roots back to this brand, which started in 1876 in the heart of Milan.

This adventurous design would never have been possible prior to manufacturing advances that enabled designs to be sublimated on to polyester.

1988
SUPER CONFEX/ YOKO/COLNAGO TEAM JERSEY

Manufacturer: Decca

Associated bike: Colnago

Key rider: Jean-Paul Van Poppel

During the late eighties, the Super Confex's lead-out train was a sight to behold, with the likes of Frans Maassen, Jelle Nijdam, and Edwig Van Hooydonck all riding for team sprinter Jean-Paul Van Poppel.

Made in Belgium by Decca, this jersey is from the team's 1988 season. The basic jersey design did not change over the years and still looks fantastic.

1988
ALFA LUM/ LEGNANO/ ECOFLAM TEAM JERSEY

Manufacturer: Sportful
Associated bike: Legnano
Key rider: Maurizio Fondriest

This jersey certainly bears a remarkable resemblance to the iconic green and red jersey of the Legnano/Pirelli team featured on page 13 (top), although this one has the added Alfa Lum and Ecoflam sponsors. It is made from 50 per cent cotton and 50 per cent polyester, something that would be considered rather unusual today.

The following year, the familiar horizontal red and white stripes arrived and it was that jersey, also made by Sportful, which introduced the likes of Djamolidine Abdoujaparov, Dimitri Konyshev, Andrei Tchmil, and Piotr Ugrumov to the professional peloton.

WORLD CHAMPION JERSEY WITH ALFA LUM/ LEGNANO/ ECOFLAM

Manufacturer: Sportful

Associated bike: Legnano

Key rider: Maurizio Fondriest

The rising star of the Alfa Lum team was the Italian Maurizio Fondriest, who performed beyond all expectations in 1988, culminating in his surprising win at the World Championship in Belgium.

Fondriest wore this World Champion jersey, made from 70 per cent cotton and 30 per cent polyester, for a number of weeks until the end of the season, but he then made a big-money move to the Del Tongo squad for 1989.

After winning the overall UCI World Cup in 1991 for Panasonic he founded a bicycle manufacturer, called Fondriest, which is still in business today.

1988
7-ELEVEN TEAM JERSEY

Manufacturer: Descente

Associated bike:
Eddy Merckx Cycles

Key rider: Andy Hampsten

While many jerseys from the period can be criticized for having too many logos and looking too busy, this jersey actually works because of all the logos.

It is a well-recognized design, perhaps due to Andy Hampsten's greatest career moment when he overcame a blizzard on the Gavia Pass during the 1988 Giro d'Italia to take the leader's jersey.

The looped-back polyester fabric was used to add extra insulation, but it doesn't work very well compared with today's super-technical yarns and fibres.

The absence of Descente cloth labels and customized zip pullers suggests that this particular version of the jersey was not made by the original manufacturer.

1989
ADR/AGRIGEL
TEAM JERSEY

Manufacturer: unknown
Associated bike: Bottecchia
Key rider: Greg LeMond

The 1989 edition of the Tour de France was probably the best for many years. By the final time trial in Paris, just 50 seconds separated Laurent Fignon, riding for Super U, and Greg LeMond, riding for ADR. LeMond won the race by a slender eight seconds and now, thanks to Lance Armstrong's results being struck from the record books, remains the only American to have ever done so.

Santini sponsored the team, but this jersey is not made by Santini. Before the days of online shopping, the only way to get a pro team kit was from a local bike shop or via mail order. Many jerseys were produced in Belgium to meet demand, and do not feature the tell-tale signs of an authentic jersey. This one does not feature Santini's logo, the zip puller is unbranded and the cloth label at the collar is also unbranded.

CHATEAU D'AX/ SALOTTI TEAM JERSEY

Manufacturer: MOA Nalini

Associated bike: F Moser

Key riders: Gianni Bugno, Tony Rominger

Gianni Bugno was an extremely versatile rider, able to win grand tours as well as the spring classics too. I was lucky enough to witness his win at the 1994 Tour of Flanders, beating local favourite Johan Museeuw on his own turf.

Unfortunately for Bugno, he lived in Miguel Indurain's shadow at the Tour de France, but he did win the 1990 Giro d'Italia, incredibly leading from start to finish!

I was a great fan of Bugno, but did not own this jersey – which he wore in 1989 while riding for Chateau d'Ax – as I didn't like the busy, logo-heavy design. I did, however, own a team-issue F Moser AX Leader bike, which I raced successfully for a number of seasons.

THE
NINETIES

||||||||||||||||||||||||||||||||||||||||||||||||||||||||||||||||||||||||||||||||||||||||||

Mario Cipollini of the Saeco team was the king of cool in the nineties. One of the greatest sprinters of all time, he constantly courted controversy with his cycling fashion statements. Turning up dressed as Julius Caesar, wearing stars-and-stripes shorts to honour his American bike sponsor Cannondale, bold Briko glasses, or at one time a skinsuit with muscles, ligaments, and sponsors' logos sublimated to the fabric, he was never dull! Although the UCI fined the team for Super Mario's stunts, they were happy to pay given the publicity it gained for their brands – this was well before social media!

By the mid-nineties, Etxeondo had started to supply their professional riders in the ONCE team with Gore-Tex rain jackets, complete with sublimated team logos, and "Roubaix" fleece-lined bib shorts for early-season races like Paris–Nice. Advancements in manufacturing were focusing more attention on the actual construction of the garment, and bib short design was one area of improvement. Santini was responsible for further developing the chamois/seat pad. In conjunction with the Mapei team, they pioneered the slim-line gel insert, which helped absorb vibration and improved the riders' comfort.

◀ Andrei Tchmil (Lotto) celebrates victory at the 1994 edition of the Paris–Roubaix wearing one of the more sophisticated jerseys to come out of the nineties. The decade was characterized by over-the-top designs resulting from advances in computer technology and manufacturing techniques.

1990
TOSHIBA TEAM JERSEY

Manufacturer: Santini
Associated bike: Look Cycle
Key riders: Jean-François Bernard, Laurent Jalabert

After the team's unique and unforgettable 1989 jersey, which was very similar to La Vie Claire jersey design (see page 46), this Toshiba design was always going to split opinion. Reminiscent of World War I dazzle camouflage, it was controversial and makes the occasional appearance on fans' "worst jersey of all time" lists. At the time of its release I didn't like it either, but in hindsight and compared with some of the cluttered modern jerseys of today, it now looks pleasantly simple.

Jean-François Bernard carried a heavy burden during his career, being the next great hope for French cycling after Bernard Hinault. His mantle has passed to his son Julien, who is hoping to find his feet in the pro peloton without the weight of a nation's expectations on his shoulders.

1991
BUCKLER/ SUNTOUR/ COLNAGO TEAM JERSEY

Manufacturer: Decca

Associated bike: Colnago

Key rider: Edwig Van Hooydonck

This is another jersey that traces its way back to the Kwantum team started in 1984, sponsored by Buckler (a low-alcohol Belgian beer) from 1990 through to 1992. WordPerfect succeeded Buckler as headline sponsor of the team in 1993, bringing a new look to the jersey (see page 72).

I was a big fan of Edwig Van Hooydonck and was delighted when Britain's Dave Rayner joined the team in 1991 to ride under the guidance of the legendary Jan Raas.

Van Hooydonck is now widely credited as the inventor of three-quarter-length bib tights, after he cut some full-length bib tights down to shorten them but still protect his knees against the elements in early-season races.

VÊTEMENT Z/CYCLES PEUGEOT/ HALFORDS TEAM JERSEY

Manufacturer: Impsport

Associated bike: none

Key rider: none

This is a British version of the cartoon-like Z-jersey, which was seen more often in Europe on the likes of Greg LeMond, Robert Millar, and Gilbert Duclos-Lassalle. Made by Impsport, this slightly more cluttered version had UK-specific sponsors added and was used when the team rode the Milk Race.

The Milk Race was a key event for UK-based riders, allowing them to test their fitness against a selection of European professionals, as well as the mighty Eastern European amateur teams. It is a role that the Aviva Tour of Britain fulfils today.

1993
GATORADE/ CHATEAU D'AX TEAM JERSEY

Manufacturer: Santini

Associated bike: Bianchi

Key riders: Gianni Bugno, Laurent Fignon

With Gianni Bugno as their undisputed leader in 1993, the Gatorade/Chateau D'Ax team also hired two-time Tour de France winner Laurent Fignon as co-leader and mentor for Bugno, to help him in his battles against Miguel Indurain.

After a poor Giro d'Italia, Fignon managed to win a stage at the Tour de France while helping Bugno to third place overall. Thanks to his victory the previous year in Stuttgart, Bugno wore the rainbow bands of World Champion during 1992, and then went on to win his second title at the end of 1992 in Benidorm.

Featuring its title sponsor's corporate colours, this jersey also rather unusually included a picture of what the sponsor actually sold – pre-mixed energy drinks – to ensure it got the message across.

1993
MOTOROLA/ EDDY MERCKX TEAM JERSEY

Manufacturer: Giordana

Associated bike:
Eddy Merckx Cycles

Key riders: Lance Armstrong,
Axel Merckx

The design of this jersey has always been a personal favourite, perhaps because the colour-coordinated Eddy Merckx MX-Leader bikes made from Columbus tubing were always popular in our house.

While in-race communication with radio is now commonplace, it was the Motorola team that broke this technology, largely thanks to the technical expertise of their main sponsor.

Though revelations of doping have brought Lance Armstrong from hero to zero in recent years, the way he broke away from the peloton into Limoges on Stage 18 of the 1995 Tour de France – which he later declared a tribute to his late team mate Fabio Casartelli – will stay with me for ever.

▶ Wearing a jersey design that still looks good today, Australian Phil Anderson and Colombian Alvaro Mejia ride at the front of the peloton aboard their Eddy Merckx bikes.

WORDPERFECT/ SUNTOUR/ COLNAGO TEAM JERSEY

Manufacturer: Decca
Associated bike: Colnago
Key rider: Eric Vanderaerden

WordPerfect took over from Buckler in 1993 as the main sponsor of this team, which could trace its origins right back to the Kwantum team of 1984.

The designers at Decca must have taken their cue from the colourful Mapei team jersey, featuring these delightful multi-coloured floppy disks on the front of the jersey.

The WordPerfect product line was sold twice, first to Novell Networks in June 1994, which meant a change of jersey design for 1995 to a more corporate and safe design.

1993
CHEVROLET/ LA SHERIFF/ LITESPEED/ GIORDANA TEAM JERSEY

Manufacturer: Giordana

Associated bike: Litespeed

Key rider: Malcolm Elliott

This colourful jersey dates back to the era of Malcolm Elliott, when he was winning races on the domestic pro circuit.

Back in the nineties when he signed for the Chevrolet/LA Sheriff cycling team, Elliot seemed to exist in a whole new world of glamour – riding the super-exotic Litespeed bikes in sunny California, driving to races in Chevrolets... In retrospect, I imagine that the reality was somewhat different, but this jersey does seem glamorous enough to keep the dream alive!

1993
CASTO/ CASTORAMA/ NALINI TEAM JERSEY

Manufacturer: MOA Nalini

Associated bike: Maxi Sports

Key rider: Jacky Durand

Until I read Laurent Fignon's biography *We Were Young and Carefree*, I often wondered who thought it would be a good idea to design a jersey like this – it's certainly a controversial one, resembling as it does the uniform worn by workers at Castorama, a popular chain of French hardware stores. However, it would appear that Laurent himself actually had a hand in the design.

This makes my own personal list of the worst jersey designs – sorry, Laurent – but it's an interesting jersey nonetheless.

1993

ZG MOBILI/ SELLE ITALIA/ BOTTECCHIA TEAM JERSEY

Manufacturer: Sportful
Associated bike: Bottecchia
Key rider: Massimo Ghirotto

The design of this colourful jersey by Sportful was masterminded by manager Gianni Savio, who is well known for his sartorial elegance.

However, the concept of a logo-laden jersey was not a deliberate design decision, but a commercial one. The theory behind it was based on stability: if you have 30 sponsors all contributing to the running of the team, it is easier to replace them if they drop out than it is to replace a single major sponsor. It's a strategy that Savio continues to implement to this day.

1994

CARRERA JEANS/ TASSONI/ GAERNE/ TONELLO PRO TEAM JERSEY

Manufacturer: MOA Nalini
Associated bike: Carrera
Key riders: Claudio Chiappucci, Marco Pantani

The matching denim-look bib shorts that accompanied this design were a heinous crime against fashion, but the jersey has stood the test of time. The one person who managed to pull off the complete kit was the late Marco Pantani.

Pantani turned professional at the end of 1992, as a stagiaire with Davide Boifava's Carrera Jeans/ Vagabond team. Although he rode the 1993 edition of the Giro d'Italia, most cycling fans will remember his epic efforts sporting this jersey in the mountain stages the following year, when he was supposed to be riding in support of the team's leader Claudio Chiappucci.

1994
TEAM TELEKOM
TEAM JERSEY

Manufacturer: Biemme

Associated bike:
Eddy Merckx Cycles

Key riders: Olaf Ludwig, Erik Zabel

Although in my opinion this jersey design is outshone by the far simpler 2001 version, it does have a link with the superb, colour-coordinated Eddy Merckx team bike with Campagnolo components, which I remember fondly.

While the team were arguably more successful when riding Pinarello bikes during the late nineties and early noughties, it was only right that with Axel Merckx on the team, they rode on his father Eddy's bikes.

German Jan Ullrich joined the team as a stagiaire in 1994, starting his journey towards an annual battle with his weight and form – and with Lance Armstrong.

HISTOR/LASER COMPUTER TEAM JERSEY

Manufacturer: Biemme

Associated bike: Look Cycle

Key rider: Wilfried Nelissen

The 1994 season is remembered for the horrific crash that saw Wilfried Nelissen colliding with a gendarme who was foolishly taking a photograph during the first road stage of the Tour de France.

Of course, Nelissen was wearing this bold Belgian National Champion's jersey at the time of the crash, which also saw Laurent Jalabert injured, sitting on the tarmac in his special-edition pink ONCE jersey.

With Nelissen out of the Tour, the Histor team battled on but ultimately without much success.

1994
COMBINATION JERSEY

Manufacturer: Giordana

Associated bike: none

Key rider: none

This jersey, which is the result of an unusual attempt by Giordana to group together the designs of several disparate teams that were active during the nineties into one jersey, was never worn.

The "combination jersey" was a strange thing for a manufacturer to create, though in 1995 this kind of compound design could have been useful when the Tour de France organizers invited a combined team – with six Team Telekom riders and three ZG Mobili riders – to the Tour. In the end, however, the combined kit idea wasn't chosen, and each rider rode in their own standard team kit throughout the event.

1994

EUSKADI/ ETXEONDO BASQUE SELECTION TEAM JERSEY

Manufacturer: Etxeondo

Associated bike: Orbea

Key rider: none

Back in 1994, the Euskadi team was self-funded by the Fundación Ciclista de Euskadi, with the help of local businesses and cycling fans. In the spirit of pulling together, the Basque clothing manufacturer Etxeondo supplied the clothing, and Orbea provided the bikes under the Zeus name.

Etxeondo were ahead of their time in terms of clothing cut, fit, and quality. With an Etxeondo-branded YKK zip puller and a breathable perforated material the jersey is still relevant today.

1995

FESTINA WATCHES/ LOTUS/ PEUGEOT/SIBILLE TEAM JERSEY

Manufacturer: Sibille

Associated bike: Peugeot

Key rider: Richard Virenque

For many, the most memorable Festina jersey is the 1998 design, which sticks in many fans' minds after the doping scandal that erupted on the eve of that year's Tour de France. The team's self-made spokesman, Richard Virenque, made headlines by breaking down in tears in front of the world's press before the team's impending implosion.

This 1995 jersey, however, comes from an earlier, happier time.

Despite the potential for bad PR after the 1998 scandal, Festina do, to their credit, still sponsor many pro bike races. In 2013 Santini produced a new Festina kit, albeit for a smaller team.

LOTTO/ ISOGLASS/ VITUS TEAM JERSEY

Manufacturer: Biemme

Associated bike: Vitus Bikes

Key rider: Andrei Tchmil

Andrei Tchmil's win in the epic 1994 Paris–Roubaix made it one of the most fascinating editions of the race. This jersey is the 1995 version of the jersey he wore, but there was very little difference between the two, apart from the bike sponsor changing from Caloi (whose bikes were actually made in the Eddy Merckx factory in Belgium) to Vitus Bikes.

The simplicity of this Lotto team jersey is striking. The bold red, black, and white colour scheme and distinctive logos looked great in the peloton.

Biemme, who manufactured this jersey, once made around 25 per cent of all pro team jerseys, yet has lost market share over the years to a number of other brands.

LE GROUPEMENT/ BIANCHI TEAM JERSEY

Manufacturer: Biemme
Associated bike: Bianchi
Key riders: Luc Leblanc, Robert Millar

The French Le Groupement/ Bianchi team was backed by a sponsor that folded halfway through the season, just before the Tour, leaving recently crowned British Champion Robert Millar and World Champion Luc Leblanc out of a job.

Le Groupement also signed Graeme Obree for the start of 1995, but the relationship ended quickly when Obree found himself at odds with the way the team operated.

This jersey design is not a popular one, and in the minds of many it is consigned to the history books as one of the worst of all time. Not even the magic of the Bianchi name could save this one! In the words of Andrew Critchlow from the *Telegraph*, "Le Groupement barely lasted a season before folding – but the legacy of its hideous cycling strip will live in memory forever."

GEWISS/ BALLAN/BIANCHI TEAM JERSEY

Manufacturer: Biemme

Associated bike: Bianchi

Key riders: Moreno Argentin, Eugeni Berzin

The Gewiss/Ballan team dominated the early-season classics in 1994 with Argentin, Berzin, and team mate Giorgio Furlan winning all before them. Berzin then won the Giro d'Italia while team mate Piotr Ugrumov came second overall in the Tour de France. Vadislav Bobrik finished the season off by winning the Giro di Lombardia.

Some at the time, perhaps naively, suggested that the team's success was down to their early adoption of Campagnolo's new aerodynamic Shamal wheels, yet evidence of systematic doping within the team has since come to light.

The jersey design has stood the test of time, however. Combined with the matching navy bib shorts, it was a great contrast to the *celeste* (sky-blue) colour of the Bianchi bikes the team rode.

1995

MERCATONE UNO/SAECO/ PINARELLO TEAM JERSEY

Manufacturer: Castelli

Associated bike: Pinarello

Key riders: Mario Cipollini, Michele Bartoli

The combined Mercatone Uno/Saeco team had 35 riders, including 5 stagiaires (new professional riders), from September 1995 – an unthinkable number these days. It was no surprise when the team later split to form two teams: Saeco/Estro (1996/1997) and Mercatone Uno/ Wega (1997).

This jersey was made by the manufacturer Castelli, who added some very nice touches, including a smart zip featuring a Castelli-branded puller. The Scorpion logo is still used by Castelli today.

1996
MAPEI/GB/ COLNAGO TEAM JERSEY

Manufacturer: Sportful

Associated bike: Colnago

Key riders: Johan Museeuw, Franco Ballerini, Andrea Tafi

The Mapei team started in 1994 as Mapei/Clas, but GB soon replaced Clas, bringing with them a contingent of riders including Johan Museeuw. This move shaped the future destiny of the team. The mighty Mapei team went on to rack up 653 victories and had an incredible roster of riders at the height of their powers.

This is a 1996 team jersey, despite the two 1995 logos showing that Mapei was the top Italian-ranked and UCI World-ranked team. At around this time, Sportful took the unusual step of producing team-issue garments for public sale. It was a rare move at the time, though it has since become common for a manufacturer to offer a replica and a pro-issue range in this way.

WORLD CHAMPION JERSEY WITH MAPEI/GB/ LATEXCO/ SPORTFUL

Manufacturer: Sportful
Associated bike: Colnago
Key rider: Abraham Olano

A fantastic World Champion jersey with Mapei/GB logos, this design was made by Sportful to celebrate Abraham Olano's win at the World Road Race Championships in 1995, which were held at altitude around Duitama, Colombia.

Olano won the title ahead of his compatriot Miguel Indurain (who was the overwhelming favourite) and Marco Pantani. Incredibly, he actually won the title on a punctured rear tube. The gap he had on the chasing pack was too small for him to change the wheel or bike, so he rode the last 2km (1¼ miles) with a softening rear tyre.

1996
CARRERA JEANS/LONGONI SPORT/GAERNE/ NALINI PRO TEAM JERSEY

Manufacturer: MOA Nalini

Associated bike: Carrera

Key riders: Claudio Chiappucci, Marco Pantani

The Giro d'Italia can make or break a team's season, and 1996 did not start well for Carrera with team superstar Pantani injured, and Chiappucci's star fading. Yet Enrico Zaina saved the day with a stage win and podium spot, and Carrera also took the team classification.

The jersey changed little from the 1994 version (see page 74) with the faux-denim bib shorts still present. Nalini resurrected this kit recently in one of their modern collections, but despite the current popularity of the retro look, those bib shorts were a step too far for most amateur riders.

1996
MG BOYS MAGLIFICIO/ TECHNOGYM/ NALINI TEAM JERSEY

Manufacturer: MOA Nalini

Associated bike: Coppi

Key riders: Fabio Baldato, Gianni Bugno

Although it was worn by two of the most popular riders of all time, this jersey design doesn't reflect the excitement and anticipation fans felt when watching them in action.

The team was a joy to watch during its heyday. Everything Bugno did on the bike seemed effortless, and without Miguel Indurain he no doubt would have won a lot more.

There is nothing remarkable about the design of this jersey, with the logos of the two title sponsors taking most of the available space, yet the diamonds at the bottom do call to mind the cubes of the Mapei team jersey (see page 83).

1996
POSTOBÓN/ MANZANA/ RYALCAO TEAM JERSEY

Manufacturer: Assos

Associated bike: Pinarello

Key rider: Luis Herrera

The Colombian Postobón team were in the peloton for ten years but were often in the shadows of the mighty Café de Colombia team.

The team had many victories and saw several wonderful riders come and go: Luis Herrera rode the last two years of his career with the team, and Chepe González began his career with them.

This bold, adventurous jersey design from Assos used the font styling of the main sponsors to provide the team with a colourful, modern look throughout the nineties.

1997
GB NATIONAL CHAMPION JERSEY WITH BANESTO/ CAMPAGNOLO

Manufacturer: MOA Nalini

Associated bike: Pinarello

Key rider: Jeremy Hunt

This is one of the most attractive GB National Champion jerseys of all time, with the national flag combining beautifully with the design of the jersey. This example is an early replica, sold in an age when champions' jerseys were incredibly hard for fans to acquire.

Hunt was a wonderful rider, who had some outstanding results as a pro – two stand-out performances being his wins at GP Ouest-France (2002) and Trofeo Alcudia (1998). I was fortunate enough to compete against a young Hunt as a junior, when he would often ride his bike the 80–95km (50–60 miles) to get to a race and then still beat us all!

1997
BELGIAN CHAMPION JERSEY WITH MAPEI/GB/ LATEXCO/ SPORTFUL

Manufacturer: Sportful

Associated bike: Colnago

Key rider: Tom Steels

Tom Steels was Belgian National Road Race Champion in 1997, 1998, 2002, and 2004. Steels was a fiery character on the bike, cementing his reputation during the 1997 Tour de France when he threw his bottle at fellow sprinter Frédéric Moncassin at the end of Stage 6.

Steels rode for the Mapei team for six years, with Sportful sponsoring the team for a number of years, too. This bold, uncluttered design evokes memories of an earlier era of cycling jerseys.

1997
ONCE/LOOK/ MAVIC/ ETXEONDO TEAM JERSEY

Manufacturer: Etxeondo

Associated bike: Look Cycle

Key riders: Laurent Jalabert, Alex Zülle

The ONCE team was quick to adopt high-tech fabrics such as Windstopper and Gore-Tex, making their riders look far more comfortable in the grim early-season conditions of races such as the Paris–Nice.

Though the striking yellow of this jersey is used to great effect, there was obvious potential for confusion with the iconic yellow leader's jersey in the Tour de France. As a result, ONCE used to swap the yellow background of the jerseys for a pink background, so that members of the team would not be confused with the leader of the race.

1997
SAECO/ESTRO/ CANNONDALE/ CODA TEAM JERSEY

Manufacturer: Cannondale

Associated bike: Cannondale

Key rider: Mario Cipollini

This jersey has stood the test of time, with a design that still looks fabulous to this day. Its bold lettering across the chest made it incredibly easy to identify the Saeco riders installing themselves at the front of the bunch in support of their team leader, Mario Cipollini. Cipollini was one of the biggest names in the peloton at the time, winning more than 60 races in 3 years.

The jerseys led to the team being nicknamed the "Red Train", though they weren't the first to have this nickname. It's been around in various forms over the years, with Rik Van Looy's "Red Guard" perhaps the first to be given it.

The team's fat-tubed, colour-coded aluminium Cannondale bikes complemented the jerseys for a great overall team look.

JAPANESE CHAMPION JERSEY WITH MAPEI/GB/ SPORTFUL

Manufacturer: Sportful
Associated bike: Colnago
Key rider: Yoshiyuki Abe

While French, Dutch, Belgian, and even GB jerseys are a common sight at the important races in the professional calendar, the Japanese Champion jersey is harder to spot.

Yoshiyuki Abe was a trailblazer in the nineties, first riding for Panaria/Vinavil and then graduating to the mighty Mapei/GB team in 1997, although you will not find any of those famous Mapei cubes on this jersey. Yoshiyuki's one and only pro win was the sixth Japan Cup in 1997.

More recently, Fumiyuki Beppu and Yukiya Arashiro have raised the profile of Japanese riders, which must be heartening to equipment sponsors like Shimano whose headquarters are in Japan.

1998
EUSKADI
ELITE BASQUE
SELECTION
TEAM JERSEY

Manufacturer: Etxeondo

Associated bike: none

Key rider: none

During televised pro races, the distinctive Basque Ikurrina flag is always on display when the road starts to climb up towards the Pyrenees, so it's a common sight for cycling fans.

This striking jersey was worn by the top amateur riders of the region, who were hoping to gain selection to the pro ranks. The kit was made by Etxeondo for many years, then Spiuk took over production for a few years, and finally it was MOA that provided the team kit for the 2014 Continental team.

ORBEA/ZEUS/ VENETO MTB TEAM JERSEY

Manufacturer: Etxeondo

Associated bike: Orbea

Key rider: none

Before Orbea became the global bicycle brand they are today, they used to market their bikes under three different names – Orbea, Zeus, and Veneto – in different territories. That's why this MTB (mountain bike) team jersey apparently has three lead sponsors.

The jersey itself was for a small Spanish MTB team, which was sponsored by Orbea and clothed by Etxeondo, with additional sponsorship provided by RockShox forks and Columbus tubing.

Etxeondo have tried to create a design that lives up to their usual elegant and cutting-edge standards. But they have had to balance that with the demands of a modern professional MTB team that needs to keep a variety of sponsors happy.

1998

MERCATONE UNO/BIANCHI TEAM JERSEY

Manufacturer: Santini

Associated bike: Bianchi

Key riders: Marco Pantani, Dimitri Konyshev

This is a replica of the jersey worn by the winner of the 1998 Giro d'Italia, Marco Pantani, made by the official team clothing supplier Santini. In order to keep the Tour de France bosses happy, the team jerseys were changed to contain less yellow so they were not confused with that race leader's yellow jersey.

The previous year's jersey had a great combination of blue and yellow but most people better remember the 1998 version, due to Marco Pantani's achievement of winning both the Giro and the Tour in the same year.

1998

SWISS CHAMPION JERSEY WITH MAPEI/BRICOBI/ LATEXCO

Manufacturer: Sportful

Associated bike: Colnago

Key rider: Oscar Camenzind

This is a replica jersey from Sportful that is based on the design worn by Swiss Champion Oscar Camenzind, while riding for the mighty Mapei team. Camenzind won the Swiss title in June 1997, but this is the jersey design he wore up until Niki Aebersold stole the title in June 1998.

While most National Champion jerseys have horizontal stripes across the chest in the colours of the nation's flag, the Swiss Champion jersey nearly always features a striking white cross on a red background.

◄ Love him or loathe him, Lance Armstrong's performance in the 1999 Tour de France was unbelievable. Here he sports a long-sleeved skinsuit of the bold US Postal Service jersey.

US POSTAL SERVICE/TREK TEAM JERSEY

Manufacturer: Pearl Izumi

Associated bike: Trek

Key riders: Lance Armstrong, George Hincapie

No European team was willing to take a chance on Armstrong in 1998, following his battle with cancer, but his links back to Thomas Weisel's Subaru/Montgomery amateur team helped him get a ride on the US Postal Service team in 1999, wearing this jersey.

From 2000 onwards, the team's jerseys were made by the sportswear giant Nike; it was inevitable that the growing international popularity of pro cycling would lead to Nike's infamous "swoosh" making an appearance in the peloton. I do feel, however, that this Pearl Izumi jersey looks far better than any of the subsequent Nike versions.

It's interesting to note that during the 1999 Tour de France, Lance Armstrong did actually wear a Nike jersey, as Nike sponsored the Tour de France leaders' jerseys that year.

THE NOUGHTIES

||||||||||||||||||||||||||||||||||||||||||||||||||||||||||||||||||||||||||||||||||||||||||||||||||||||

The fairytale comeback of Lance Armstrong from cancer brought many new sponsors to cycling during the early part of the decade – often organizations with big marketing budgets. The cost of sponsoring a top-level professional team soared, which meant companies already in the industry, including traditional clothing manufacturers like Nalini, had to slim down their pro team rosters. This trend has continued into the present day, with most companies focusing their marketing effort into an ever-smaller number of teams.

Another external factor to affect the cycling industry was the boom in e-commerce. Companies like Geoffrey Butler and Prendas had previously been mail order specialists, but e-commerce opened up the market and made it far easier for fans to buy their favourite team's jersey.

While sublimation well and truly arrived in the eighties, the noughties brought with them the use of digital screen printers which enabled the personalization of cycling garments. Little details, like rider names and national flags on the side panels of a jersey, were impossible with an offset press, but digital printing allowed some much-needed flexibility.

This had a knock-on effect on small local cycling clubs, who were previously unable to get a custom kit made for only five or ten riders. The flexibility of digital printers allowed an unlimited number of colours to be used for each personalized print, albeit at a higher unit cost.

◀ Brash, over-confident, cocky... all words that have been thrown at Mark Cavendish. His brutally honest comments in post-race interviews often make his press officers cringe, but they give a great insight into the split-second decisions involved in modern bunch sprinting.

2000
EUSKALTEL/ EUSKADI TEAM JERSEY

Manufacturer: Etxeondo
Associated bike: Orbea
Key riders: Roberto Laiseka, Samuel Sánchez

Whenever I wear this jersey I remember just what a great fit it is. Although the seat pad in the matching bib shorts is somewhat lacking compared with the elastic seat pads of today, the jersey still feels good – even after all these years!

It is easy to tell this is a 2000 version of the jersey because of the placement of the Orbea logo and, more obviously, the turquoise Euskaltel lettering; it was white from 2004 onwards. See also the 2008 "Pays Basque" version of the team's jersey on page 146, and the 2011 version on page 184 made by Italian manufacturer MOA.

2000
KELME/COSTA BLANCA/ EUROSPORT TEAM JERSEY

Manufacturer: MOA Nalini

Associated bike: Look Cycle

Key riders: Santiago Botero, Roberto Heras

For the 2000 season, the Kelme/Costa Blanca/Eurosport team were given a selection wildcard by the Tour de France organizers, and they wore this fetching green, blue, and white jersey for the race.

The team was well known for its performances in the mountains, and Fernando Escartín was tipped for a place in the top ten – which he duly achieved. But the team surpassed all expectations by winning the team classification; Botero won the King of the Mountains jersey as well as a stage; and Javier Otxoa also took a stage, beating Lance Armstrong to the mountain-top finish at Hautacam.

Javier Otxoa was badly injured in an accident in 2001, but he took part in the 2004 Athens Paralympics and went on to win the CP3 road race.

2000
LINDA McCARTNEY TEAM JERSEY

Manufacturer: Giordana

Associated bike: Principia

Key riders: Pascal Richard, Max Sciandri

This version of the Linda McCartney Foods team kit, made in Italy by Giordana, closely resembled the sponsor's product packaging at the time. With hardly any other sponsors on the jersey, there was plenty of space for the Linda McCartney logos, creating maximum effect on the bike and podiums.

The team were lucky to get a wildcard entry into the 2000 edition of the Giro d'Italia. Matt Stephens (who now works for the Global Cycling Network) won over many Italian hearts during the race by trying his very best to keep going while injured after a crash. However, the highlight of the race had to be Australian David McKenzie taking Stage 7 with a solo breakaway, more than justifying his selection.

2001
LINDA MCCARTNEY/ JAGUAR/JACOB'S CREEK TEAM JERSEY

Manufacturer: Etxeondo

Associated bike: Principia

Key riders: David McKenzie, Bradley Wiggins

After three years of steady progress, the team had a good start in 2001 with a stage win by David McKenzie in the Tour Down Under, wearing his new-look kit by Etxeondo. The jersey marked a real departure of style, with Etxeondo expertly combining the logos of Linda McCartney, Jaguar, and Jacob's Creek on to the standard jersey as well as John Tanner's champion jersey.

However, the team then went into free-fall with news that none of the sponsors had formally agreed terms with the team management. The unfortunate riders – including future 2012 Tour de France winner Bradley Wiggins, who was just starting his career – were left without jobs.

GB NATIONAL CHAMPION JERSEY WITH LINDA MCCARTNEY/ JACOB'S CREEK

Manufacturer: Etxeondo

Associated bike: Principia

Key rider: John Tanner

The design of a national champion jersey is set by a series of rules and regulations defined by the country's national federation, and has to be approved by the UCI. Most Great British Champion jerseys have followed a very similar design of a white background with horizontal bands across the chest, and smaller bands on the collar and sleeve cuffs.

This jersey was made for John Tanner, the 2000 National Champion. Yet Tanner never got to wear this jersey design because his team was disbanded. This example has never been worn because it is so small. Most fans underestimate just how lean professional cyclists are.

2001
CANTINA TOLLO/ ACQUA & SAPONE TEAM JERSEY

Manufacturer: MOA Nalini
Associated bike: Olmo Bikes
Key rider: Danilo Di Luca

This jersey was made in 2001, the final year that Cantina Tollo was the lead sponsor for the team. Secondary sponsor Acqua & Sapone took the lead in 2002 and the team, centred around Mario Cipollini, wore an extremely loud zebra-striped kit.

This 2001 version is without question a more refined affair, the design having evolved from the 1996 kit. The oval logo of Cantina Tollo sits in the centre, with the Acqua & Sapone logo and its associated "bubbles" underneath. The Longoni Sport logo here can also be seen on the 1996 Carrera Jeans jersey (see page 85).

ITALIAN NATIONAL TEAM JERSEY WITH COLNAGO/ SPORTFUL

Manufacturer: Sportful

Associated bike: Colnago

Key riders: Mario Cipollini, Paolo Bettini

This iconic version of the Italian team kit, with its classic *azzurro* colour and a great team sponsor in Colnago, was worn by Mario Cipollini when he won the 2002 World Road Championships, thanks to an incredible sprint at the Zolder motor racing circuit in Belgium. Winning the rainbow jersey at the end of 256km (159 miles) was the icing on the cake for what was arguably Cipollini's best season.

Cipo had already won Milano–San Remo, Gent Wevelgem and six Giro d'Italia stages, among other events. But what surprised fans was the way the coach, Franco Ballerini, coerced the difficult-to-manage Italian team into uniting behind Cipollini.

2002
TEAM CSC/ TISCALI TEAM JERSEY

Manufacturer: Castelli

Associated bike: Look Cycle

Key riders: Julian Dean, Tyler Hamilton

This is an early and rather simple example of the Team CSC jersey, which was seen in the peloton before later manufacturers added their embellishments. In 2003, Girodana added the "six-pack" design elements, then Descente added the classy pinstripes in 2008.

This example is marked with Julian Dean's surname on the reverse, something that is now common on pro team jerseys. In fact, when Rapha recently started supplying Team Sky with their kit, they actually allowed a small number of fans to buy replica versions of the team kit with their own name and nationality flag printed on the side panels.

In 2002 Fränk Schleck began his pro career as a stagiaire with this team, managed by Bjarne Riis, riding for nine seasons before helping to set up the Leopard Trek team in 2011.

2002
TEAM COAST/ BIANCHI PRO TEAM JERSEY

Manufacturer: Biemme

Associated bike: Bianchi

Key rider: Alex Zülle

Apart from Aitor Garmendia and his stage win in the Volta a Catalunya, Alex Zülle was Team Coast/Bianchi's biggest star in 2002. With wins in the Tour de Suisse, Tour de Romandie, Vuelta Ciclista a la Comunidad Valenciana, and the Volta ao Algarve, the accident-prone Swiss star took most of the team's victories that year.

The multi-coloured Coast logo did lack impact on the 2002 all-yellow jersey design. Being predominately yellow, like Zülle's previous ONCE team jersey, the background of this jersey would have had to be changed for the Tour de France, but the team was not selected and, in fact, folded at the end of 2003.

2002
GIRO D'ITALIA OVERALL LEADER'S JERSEY

Manufacturer: Santini

Associated bike: none

Key rider: Cadel Evans

This replica jersey celebrates Cadel Evans's time in the Maglia Rosa (the overall leader's jersey) during the 2002 Giro d'Italia.

Evans took hold of the Maglia Rosa on the tour only to lose it the next day in a heart-breaking collapse. He then had to wait until 2010 to wear a leader's jersey again.

It is unusual to get a replica jersey with sponsor panels printed at the factory, but as Santini sponsor both the team and the jersey competition in the race, they have the rights to produce a jersey with sponsor panels for replica sales after the event.

2003
TEAM COAST/ BIANCHI PRO TEAM JERSEY

Manufacturer: Etxeondo

Associated bike: Bianchi

Key riders: Jan Ullrich, Alex Zülle

This is one of my favourite Etxeondo jerseys and one of the most beautiful in my collection. The team started the season in a mainly blue jersey, but this *celeste* version was issued to the team in time for the 2003 Giro d'Italia.

The team's bike sponsor, Bianchi, took over the reins as main sponsor when Coast stopped paying the riders' wages in April. Nalini took over the sponsorship of the team clothing, producing a retro-looking jersey for Jan Ullrich and his team mates.

Ullrich had his best Tour de France performance in 2003, giving Lance Armstrong a really hard time in the overall classification.

2003
UKRAINIAN NATIONAL CHAMPION JERSEY WITH DE NARDI/COLPACK

Manufacturer: Santini

Associated bike: Coppi

Key rider: Serhiy Honchar

This colourful and unusual jersey was made to celebrate Serhiy Honchar's National Championship win. It was made by Santini, who were the team clothing sponsor for De Nardi/Colpack at the time.

Honchar was known for his messy, yet very effective style on the bike, often turning over a huge gear compared with his competitors. Honchar was the Ukrainian National Road Champion in 2003 and was five-times National Time Trial Champion, as well as the World Time Trial Champion in 2000. He retired in 2010 when he was unable to find a team.

2003
GB/WORLD CLASS NATIONAL TEAM JERSEY

Manufacturer: Impsport

Associated bike: none

Key rider: none

When lime green appeared on the GB National Team jersey in 2003, complaints to the British Cycling Federation were pretty vocal! There were also a number of letters to the cycling press, who were happy to publish the furious words of their readers.

It was team member Julian Winn who came up with the design, but after three or four years global clothing giant Adidas took over from Impsport, and they reverted to a more traditional red, white, and blue for the team's colours.

2003
GIRO D'ITALIA OVERALL LEADER'S JERSEY

Manufacturer: Santini

Associated bike: none

Key rider: none

The design of an iconic race leader's jersey does not usually change much over time. Since it was first introduced in 1931, the Maglia Rosa has become an iconic symbol of Italian cycling and the Giro d'Italia.

In 2003, however, the race organizers decided to do something a little different by commissioning Italian painter and sculptor Ugo Nespolo to design the backdrop of the 86th edition jersey. By revising their previous conservative approach to the Maglia Rosa the organizers created an artistic, adventurous and innovative design which prompted much renewed interest in the jersey.

2004
UCI WORLD CUP OVERALL LEADER'S JERSEY

Manufacturer: Santini

Associated bike: none

Key rider: none

The UCI Road World Cup was an excellent event for the one-day specialists in the peloton. The season-long competition comprised a number of events – mainly the spring and autumn classics – with points allocated for finishing in the top 25.

From 1989, a jersey was designed for the leader so he could be clearly identified in the peloton. The jersey had to be distinct from the rainbow jersey of the current World Champion. So instead of the horizontal bands of the World Champion jersey, the World Cup jersey had vertical bands of colour on a white background. More often than not they were all but covered by the front and rear sponsor panels.

At the end of the 2004 season, the competition was replaced by the UCI ProTour.

2004
GB NATIONAL CHAMPION JERSEY WITH MR BOOKMAKER/ PALMANS/ COLLSTROP

Manufacturer: Vermarc

Associated bike: Ridley

Key rider: Roger Hammond

Roger Hammond's performance, which earned him third place in the Paris–Roubaix, was a highlight of the 2004 season. After years of battling in Belgium, he finally made a major breakthrough in a race that suited his cyclo-cross background.

Vermarc took no risks with the design of this jersey, although they did supply Hammond with matching white bib shorts which most national champions now shy away from.

After riding for others at Lance Armstrong's Discovery Channel team in 2005/6, Hammond had more success at Team High Road (2007/8), Cervélo TestTeam (2009/10), and finally Garmin/Cervélo (2011).

2004
US CHAMPION JERSEY WITH ACQUA & SAPONE/CAFFE MOKAMBO

Manufacturer: Santini

Associated bike: F Moser

Key rider: Freddie Rodriguez

You will no doubt notice more than a passing resemblance between this jersey and the 1977 Brooklyn wool jersey featured on page 22 and worn by Roger De Vlaeminck.

US champion Freddie Rodriguez was a big fan of De Vlaeminck, so when Santini made him this special version of his team kit, Rodriguez was delighted by how close they were able to get to the original.

During his career, Rodriguez rode for some big teams like Mapei and Lotto. While racing with some lower-division teams in the USA at the age of 39, he caused a stir by winning the 2013 National Championships, his fourth national title.

2004
FASSA BORTOLO/ PINARELLO TEAM JERSEY

Manufacturer: MOA Nalini

Associated bike: Pinarello

Key riders: Fabian Cancellara, Filippo Pozzato

Team manager Giancarlo Ferretti must have been very pleased with his star rider Alessandro Petacchi after the 2004 Giro d'Italia, in which he wore this jersey. With a remarkable nine stage victories to his name in a single edition of the race, Petacchi also won the points, combative, and the unusual Azzurri d'Italia classification.

Their success continued with the team's stage victories in the Tour de France, thanks to Cancellara, Pozzato, and Aitor González, then Petacchi went on to win four stages in the Vuelta a España. The team eventually folded at the end of 2005.

Manufacturers Nalini were lucky when creating this jersey that the number of sponsors was kept to a minimum, enabling them to come up with a bright, appealing and modern design.

2004
GIRO D'ITALIA OVERALL LEADER'S JERSEY

Manufacturer: Santini
Associated bike: none
Key rider: none

Following on from the previous year's success, RCS Sport, who organize the Giro d'Italia, commissioned Mark Kostobi to create an image to incorporate into the design of the Maglia Rosa.

Kostobi was a prolific artist; he also designed the *Use Your Illusion* album covers for Guns 'N' Roses, as well as numerous products including a Swatch watch, a bag for Bloomingdales, Alessi vases, and Rosenthal espresso cups.

The resulting jersey design is chic, modern and appealing.

2004
GIRO D'ITALIA OVERALL LEADER'S JERSEY

Manufacturer: Santini
Associated bike: Cannondale
Key rider: Damiano Cunego

Damiano Cunego did not start the Giro as Saeco's team leader; that was supposed to be defending champion Gilberto Simoni. But the young sensation stole the show, which didn't go down too well. Cunego claimed his first (and only) tour victory, taking four stage wins along the way to winning this jersey, the design of which reflects that of the jersey above, but this time with sponsor logos.

Niche DVDs made that year offer some fascinating behind-the-scenes footage of the race. Those featuring Simoni and his Saeco team mates, make for interesting viewing given the politics of the team at the time.

BELGIAN CHAMPION JERSEY WITH LANDBOUW-KREDIET/ COLNAGO/SACLA

Manufacturer: Vermarc

Associated bike: Colnago

Key rider: Tom Steels

This jersey was made as a replica for fans after Tom Steels won the Belgian nationals in 2004. It is interesting to note that the logos of two of the sub-sponsors – Colnago and Olympus – have far more prominence than that of the team's main sponsor, Landbouwkrediet.

Steels retired from professional racing at the end of the 2008 season, having ridden his very last season with Landbouwkrediet after a stint with Davitamon/ Lotto in 2005–7. The Steels name did continue in the pro peloton, however, with Tom's nephew Stijn Steels riding as a pro cyclist with Topsport Vlaanderen/Baloise.

2004
JOHAN MUSEEUW LION OF FLANDERS CELEBRATION JERSEY

Manufacturer: Vermarc

Associated bike: Time

Key rider: Johan Museeuw

Johan Museeuw's performance in the spring classics was always incredible and this celebration jersey lists all of the major victories on the front and back. The jersey was a commercial exercise by Vermarc rather than an official race item, so sadly was never worn by Museeuw.

After starting out as a bunch sprinter with ADR in 1988, Museeuw's victory in the 1993 Tour of Flanders set him on course to earn the "Lion of Flanders" nickname. Museeuw was a World Champion, World Cup winner, and won 11 monuments (the most prestigious one-day races) in all.

2004
PAOLO BETTINI OLYMPIC CELEBRATION JERSEY

Manufacturer: Vermarc

Associated bike: Time

Key rider: Paolo Bettini

Paolo Bettini took a great many victories in his pro career, but surely one of the most important was in the 2004 Athens Olympic road race when he broke away with Sérgio Paulinho for a comfortable victory. Due to the incredibly strict Olympic licensing rules, the Olympic rings never appeared on his team jersey because none of the companies that sponsored the team also sponsored the Olympics.

To right the balance, Vermarc made this "celebration" jersey, which allowed him to stand out in the peloton. Vermarc also made it available for replica sales, so Bettini fans could buy their own.

2005
COLOMBIA/SELLE ITALIA TEAM JERSEY

Manufacturer: Santini

Associated bike: Daccordi

Key riders: Iván Parra, José Rujano

After starting out with the Colombia team in 2003, José Rujano went on to have his best-ever season in 2005, taking the penultimate stage of the Giro d'Italia to Sestriere, and winning the mountains classification as well as the combativity award. Iván Parra, younger brother of Fabio Parra, took two stages in that year's Giro, too, further cementing the team's success.

The design of the team jersey from 2002 to 2005 featured a striking band with the colours of the Colombian national flag. The 2002 version was perhaps the most attractive due to its yellow background, which was dropped in 2003. Selle Italia became the team's headline sponsor in 2006, with Serramenti Diquigiovanni becoming a sub-sponsor.

2005
LIQUIGAS/ BIANCHI TEAM JERSEY WITH WORLD CHAMPION BANDS

Manufacturer: Santini

Associated bike: Bianchi

Key rider: Mario Cipollini

Mario Cipollini won the World Championships in 2002 and, as per UCI regulations, he is thereafter entitled to sport rainbow bands on his jersey collar and sleeve cuffs. This jersey was commissioned by Prendas Ciclismo to allow fans of "Super Mario" to enjoy his season with the Italian super-team Liquigas/Bianchi.

The colour scheme of the team's kit was a combination of the two lead sponsors' corporate colour palettes, though the idea of pairing the jersey with all-green leg warmers came from Mario himself. Thankfully some riders were able to adopt more tasteful navy accessories later in the season.

2005
UCI PROTOUR LEADER'S JERSEY WITH LIQUIGAS/BIANCHI

Manufacturer: Santini

Associated bike: Bianchi

Key rider: Danilo Di Luca

In 2005, Italian Danilo Di Luca started his UCI ProTour campaign well with a stage win and overall victory in the Tour of the Basque Country. Di Luca then won the Amstel Gold and the Flèche Wallonne, allowing him to wear this, the ProTour leader's white jersey.

As Santini sponsored both the UCI ProTour and the Liquigas-Bianchi team, they were able to commercialize this ProTour leader's jersey with all of the correct sponsor panel logos. Interestingly, the flash of red brought by the heart logo of Italian fashion brand Sweet Years was only on the jersey during the Giro and was replaced with an additional SMS logo for the remainder of the season.

2005
CCC POLSAT/ ORBEA/SANTINI PRO TEAM JERSEY

Manufacturer: Santini

Associated bike: Orbea

Key rider: none

Founded in 2000 in Poland, the CCC Polsat team has enjoyed a moderate amount of success right from the start.

The bold orange colour has been a constant in the design of their jerseys, and the overall look hasn't changed much over the years. Along with those of the Euskaltel team, this jersey really stands out in the peloton.

2005
SPANISH CHAMPION JERSEY WITH SAUNIER DUVAL/ PRODIR/SCOTT

Manufacturer: Santini

Associated bike: Scott

Key rider: Juan Manuel Gárate

This traditional and tasteful Spanish Champion jersey was made by Santini for Juan Manuel Gárate when he rode for Saunier Duval in 2005.

Spanish Champion jerseys of more recent years, from the Caisse d'Epargne/Movistar team, have mirrored the design of the team jersey, but with added red and yellow elements. This design is more like the classic National Champion jerseys of years gone by, a more classy affair that Gárate would look good in today.

Being a former National Champion, Gárate is entitled to have the national stripes on the collar and sleeve cuffs of any further team jerseys he wears.

TOUR DE FRANCE OVERALL LEADER'S JERSEY

Manufacturer: Nike

Associated bike: Trek

Key rider: Lance Armstrong

This yellow jersey is an officially licensed replica made in Italy (by Giordana for Nike) with the Discovery Channel sponsor panel printed at the factory.

Armstrong was, of course, subsequently stripped of his seven Tour de France titles, so there is an argument to be made for not celebrating the jersey he wore in 2005. It is, however, a fine-looking jersey, and in my opinion still worthy of featuring in this collection on its own merit, without being tarnished by wider discussions of foul play.

2005
GIRO D'ITALIA OVERALL LEADER'S JERSEY

Manufacturer: Santini

Associated bike: none

Key rider: none

In 2005, Marco Lodola designed the background design for the 88th Maglia Rosa. Lodola's original artwork had more of a neon feel to it, but it was toned down to blend in with the demands of a more international Giro than ever before.

Of all the specially commissioned designs for the Maglia Rosa, this is one of my favourites. On the replica jersey the rider can be seen clearly, but on the pro version, virtually the entire design is obscured by a white sponsor panel across the chest.

2005
GIRO D'ITALIA KING OF THE MOUNTAINS JERSEY

Manufacturer: Santini

Associated bike: none

Key rider: José Rujano

José Rujano is an out-and-out mountain climber from Venezuela. Weighing around 50kg (110lb) when in race shape, he takes an almost incomprehensible XXS size jersey.

This green King of the Mountains jersey, featuring the same Marco Lodola background design as the 88th Maglia Rosa (see page 123), is a replica made in Italy by Santini, importantly with the team sponsor panel printed at the factory. The jerseys were made for both retail sales and for the classification's sponsor.

Rujano first wore the King of the Mountains jersey after Stage 5 of the 2005 Giro, and despite Koldo Gil winning Stage 7 and wrestling the jersey off his back for four stages, Rujano was back in it until the race finish in Milan.

2005
ANDREA TAFI CELEBRATION JERSEY

Manufacturer: Santini

Associated bike: Scott

Key rider: Andrea Tafi

This eye-catching jersey design was made to celebrate Andrea Tafi's final appearance in the 2005 Paris–Roubaix. The design incorporates a graphic of the cobblestones that feature in the famous race.

It was touching that the team tried to pay tribute to Tafi's herculean efforts in the race, but although he was a former winner, Tafi sadly didn't have the same form as in his Mapei years. Perhaps it was a case of one race too many.

2005
CRÉDIT AGRICOLE/LOOK TEAM JERSEY

Manufacturer: MOA Nalini

Associated bike: Look Cycle

Key riders: Bradley Wiggins, Thor Hushovd

This Crédit Agricole pro team jersey was made for riders like Bradley Wiggins, Jaan Kirsipuu, Thor Hushovd, and Sébastien Hinault for the 2005 season.

With three rear pockets and a 14-cm (5½-inch) zip, and made from a breathable fabric, this is now a modern classic. The overall design didn't change too much over the years. It was only the introduction of the UCI ProTour logo in 2006 that brought about some minor changes around the zip.

The matching bib shorts were plain green and, while they looked okay on the pro riders, they were a disaster on most amateur fans.

SELLE ITALIA/ SERRAMENTI/ PVC DIQUIGIOVANNI TEAM JERSEY

Manufacturer: *Santini*

Associated bike: *Corratec*

Key riders: José Rujano, Wladimir Belli

It's always interesting to track the changes in sponsors over the years when you have a variety of jerseys from one team (see pages 74 top, 117, 144, 165 and 186).

As mentioned previously (see page 74), team-owner Gianni Savio has long believed that having a large number of smaller sponsors gives him more financial security for his cycling team than relying on three or four big sponsors. Although this team is not in the upper echelons of the European peloton, Savio's teams are almost certainly guaranteed a place at the Giro d'Italia – a must for any Italian sponsor. Santini have happily been involved with the team for longer than most.

CAISSE D'EPARGNE/ ILLES BALEARS TEAM JERSEY

Manufacturer: MOA Nalini

Associated bike: Pinarello

Key riders: Joaquim Rodríguez, Alejandro Valverde

This is a classy jersey – black and red is always commercially popular – and the team kept this basic look for five years. They had two jersey designs: while riding in Spain they wore one with Illes Balears's logo at the top; while riding elsewhere the Caisse d'Epargne logo was most prominent.

Another very long-running cycling team, Caisse d'Epargne/Illes Balears trace their origins back to the Reynolds team, with Banesto, Caisse, and Movistar taking the lead sponsorship role over the years.

Miguel Indurain won five Tour de France titles with the team, and in 2006 team member Óscar Pereiro was also awarded the title after Floyd Landis was stripped of it following positive drug tests.

2006
LIQUIGAS/ BIANCHI COOLMAX MESH TEAM JERSEY

Manufacturer: Santini

Associated bike: Bianchi

Key riders: Stefano Garzelli, Charly Wegelius

While the design of this jersey is similar to the 2005 version (see page 118), apart from Bianchi being demoted from the main panel to a minor sponsor position, a different fabric is used to make it.

Although most pro riders appear to wear the same short-sleeve jerseys much of the time, the fabrics they are made from can vary wildly depending on the conditions in which they are being used. With snow often a feature in the early season races and high temperatures in the summer, clothing sponsors may supply riders with as many as five different weights of jersey.

This Liquigas jersey is made from a Coolmax open mesh, which would have helped the riders stay cool when temperatures soared.

2006
FRENCH NATIONAL CHAMPION JERSEY WITH CAISSE D'EPARGNE/ ILLES BALEARS

Manufacturer: MOA Nalini

Associated bike: Pinarello

Key rider: Florent Brard

This jersey was made by Nalini for Florent Brard. It is a good example of how some manufacturers try to keep both the National Federation and the team sponsors happy by producing something a little different to the usual tricolore design, while still respecting the national colours.

Former National Champion and current manager of the FDJ team, Marc Madiot, adores the French National Champion jersey, and refuses to allow any sponsor's logos to appear on it when one of his riders has it – such as Arnaud Démare in 2014.

2006
AUSTRALIAN COMMONWEALTH GAMES TEAM JERSEY

Manufacturer: Adidas

Associated bike: none

Key rider: Anna Meares

The Australian National Team topped the medals table at the 2006 Commonwealth Games in Melbourne, claiming seven gold, five silver, and three bronze medals.

The Commonwealth Games has similar, very strict rules to the Olympic Games relating to product endorsement and sponsorship. This rather plain kit was made by Adidas, the official team supplier.

Santini have now been partners with the Australian National Team for well over ten years, and most fans will be familiar with the Santini-branded kit. It was a little strange to see the likes of Anna Meares in an Adidas jersey.

2006
JELLY BELLY/ ORBEA/ ARAMARK/ GATORADE TEAM JERSEY

Manufacturer: Santini

Associated bike: Orbea

Key rider: none

Etxeondo first made this colourful kit in 2003, but they were replaced by Santini as the team's kit supplier in 2004. Santini adopted a similar design, but with a red background, which changed to white in 2005 and green in 2006. The green jersey, with the fabulous jelly beans, helped the team stand out in the peloton in both local and national races in the USA.

The Jelly Belly bib shorts were black, making them a little more conservative than the jersey, but they still featured the colourful beans on a side panel.

The team's sock supplier, DeFeet, made an impressive effort by squeezing a number of jelly beans on to the cuffs of the socks.

2006
KAZAKHSTAN CHAMPION JERSEY WITH LIBERTY SEGUROS/ WURTH

Manufacturer: Etxeondo

Associated bike: BH Bikes

Key rider: Alexandre Vinokourov

This is a stunning kit from Etxeondo (as you would expect from the revered Basque manufacturer). The combination of cyan and yellow, however, was just a little too much for some people to take, so it is rarely seen outside the professional scene despite replicas being available for fans to buy. The matching bib shorts, in particular, are too bright for many!

2006
LIBERTY SEGUROS/ WURTH PRO TEAM JERSEY

Manufacturer: Etxeondo

Associated bike: BH Bikes

Key riders: Alberto Contador, Roberto Heras

On 25 May 2006, Liberty Mutual pulled out as primary sponsors of this team following the infamous scandal "Operación Puerto" and its claims of systematic doping.

Etxeondo subsequently provided a number of different kit designs with various sponsor names withdrawn, but eventually even they ran out of patience as they supplied the popular Euskaltel team at the time, too.

This dark blue jersey was a commendable design, however, somehow managing to look fairly uncluttered despite the various sponsors' logos.

2006
TEAM CSC GIRO D'ITALIA CELEBRATION JERSEY

Manufacturer: Descente

Associated bike: Cervélo

Key rider: Ivan Basso

After winning the team time trial with his CSC team mates, Ivan Basso went on to win Stage 8 of the Giro on his own. He then became unbelievably dominant in the final week of the race, beating his main rivals to win Stages 16 and 20 along the way to take the overall victory.

This eye-catching jersey by Descente was made to celebrate Basso's win in that event. It is, in fact, not an officially licensed leader's jersey – they are made by Santini – but it's a good attempt at creating a celebration jersey without infringing any commercial agreements.

2006
ISLE OF MAN COMMONWEALTH GAMES TEAM JERSEY

Manufacturer: Santini

Associated bike: none

Key rider: Mark Cavendish

Mark Cavendish rode for the Isle of Man in the Commonwealth Games, lapping the field in the scratch race with three other riders: Rob Hayles (ENG), Ashley Hutchinson (AUS), and James McCallum (SCO). Hayles led out for the sprint, but Cavendish went on to win gold for the Isle of Man.

Although Mark Cavendish did eventually win the UCI Road World Championships in 2011, the reason why this jersey has the rainbow bands of a former World Champion is that he won the World Madison title with Rob Hayles in 2005.

Cavendish did not wear this exact jersey in the Commonwealth Games; he wore a plain Isle of Man kit as UCI rules dictate that he could only wear his rainbow-banded version in a Madison.

GIRO D'ITALIA OVERALL LEADER'S JERSEY

Manufacturer: Santini
Associated bike: Bianchi
Key rider: none

This leader's jersey from the 2006 Giro d'Italia is a replica that was made in Italy by Santini with the Liquigas/Bianchi sponsor panel printed at the factory.

Perhaps unsurprisingly, Italian fans hold the Giro in the highest regard. There is even a museum of cycling in the north of the country, the Ghisallo Museum located on top of the Madonna del Ghisallo, a climb which has tested many Giro riders over the years. The museum honours the national tour with an incredible collection of jerseys, and aims to obtain a Maglia Rosa from every edition in the race's history.

▶ Ivan Basso (CSC) leads Danilo di Luca (Liquigas) during the Giro d'Italia. Di Luca wears the Maglia Rosa (pink jersey) to indicate that he is the race leader.

2006
GIRO D'ITALIA OVERALL LEADER'S JERSEY

Manufacturer: Santini

Associated bike: none

Key rider: none

The Maglia Rosa leader's jersey from the 89th edition of the Giro featured Lucio Del Pezzo's striking design. This was the first year the EstaTHÉ logo (the official race sponsor) appeared on the jersey. The logo became synonymous with the Giro over the next few years until it was replaced by Balocco in 2013.

EstaTHÉ used their association with the Giro to maximum effect by giving out tasty samples of their iced tea products at start and finish towns throughout the race.

2007
GIRO D'ITALIA POINTS JERSEY

Manufacturer: Santini

Associated bike: none

Key rider: none

The 2007 Giro d'Italia was the 90th edition of the legendary race, and this vibrant points jersey is a replica made in Italy by Santini.

The points competition is usually dominated by sprinters because points are awarded to the first riders over the line at the end of each stage, and to the top three at a number of intermediate sprints throughout the stage. The winner of the points classification is the rider with the most points, whereas the overall leader's classification is based on time.

2007
GIRO D'ITALIA POINTS JERSEY

Manufacturer: Santini

Associated bike: Colnago

Key rider: Alessandro Petacchi

Despite the two contrasting bold colours in its design, this jersey is a real pleasure to look at.

In 2007, a slightly darker version of *ciclamino* (mauve) was chosen for the points jersey, which is nicely complemented by the white piping on the mesh side panels. The classification sponsor Gioco Sicuro's logo neatly brings the Italian flag's colours to the jersey.

2007
GIRO D'ITALIA OVERALL LEADER'S JERSEY

Manufacturer: Santini

Associated bike: none

Key rider: none

Antonio Tamburro's painting was subtly printed on the leaders' jerseys of the 90th edition of the Giro d'Italia. Tamburro's artwork was applied to the jersey design for the four different leaders' jerseys: pink (overall), white (young riders), green (mountains), and *ciclamino* (points).

The colours of the leaders' jerseys remained the same until 2010 when the organizers replaced the *ciclamino* jersey with a red jersey. For many, this made perfect sense, with the three minor jerseys making up the colours of the national flag.

In 2012, however, the green jersey was replaced by a blue jersey to keep a new sponsor happy.

2007
GIRO D'ITALIA OVERALL LEADER'S PRO JERSEY

Manufacturer: Santini

Associated bike: Cannondale

Key rider: Danilo Di Luca

Danilo Di Luca is no saint, given his controversial history with allegations of using and abusing, but he is still listed as a winner of the 2007 edition of the Giro. This is, of course, a controversial decision, given that Alessandro Petacchi has been struck from the records, but Di Luca remains.

This jersey shows how a sponsor's panel can almost entirely obscure a design – in this instance, Antonio Tamburro's work.

2007
TOUR OF GERMANY OVERALL LEADER'S JERSEY

Manufacturer: Santini

Associated bike: none

Key rider: none

This is a replica of the 2007 Tour of Germany leader's jersey, made in Italy by Santini. It's interesting to note that Garmin sponsored this jersey before eventually becoming headline sponsor of the Garmin/Cannondale cycling team.

After the 2008 edition of the race, race organizers Upsolut decided to stop promoting the event, which was a huge loss to cycling in Germany. They do, however, still run the successful Vattenfall Cyclassics in Hamburg, which caters for 22,000 amateur cyclists and does help support the pro race scene.

2007
UCI PROTOUR DI LUCA SPECIAL EDITION JERSEY

Manufacturer: Santini

Associated bike: Cannondale

Key rider: Danilo Di Luca

Danilo Di Luca won the UCI's ProTour series in 2005 so Santini made this special edition jersey for him to wear the following season.

National and World Champions have long had the right to add stripes to their jersey collars and sleeve cuffs to denote that they are former champions, but this was the first time that a winner of a series classification was honoured in this way.

The design has never been made available for fans to buy.

2007
BARLOWORLD/ CANNONDALE TEAM JERSEY

Manufacturer: Cannondale

Associated bike: Cannondale

Key riders: Mauricio Soler, Geraint Thomas

Managed by Claudio Corti, the Barloworld Pro Continental team enjoyed a good Tour de France in 2007. Team leader Mauricio Soler took Stage 9 and the King of the Mountains title, and team mate Robbie Hunter won Stage 11.

The team also included Geraint Thomas. It was his first time riding in the Tour and he was the youngest rider competing in the race, which started in London.

Ben Swift joined the team later in the season as a stagiaire, winning the King of the Mountains title in the Tour of Britain, while Chris Froome joined in 2008, gaining valuable experience on his way to becoming a multiple Tour de France winner.

This sharp and elegant design is fantastic, helped by its minimal lines and the strong, bold font of Barloworld's corporate logo.

2008
GIRO D'ITALIA
POINTS JERSEY

Manufacturer: Santini

Associated bike: Cannondale

Key rider: Daniele Bennati

Daniele Bennati first hit the pro scene in 2002, riding for Mario Cipollini's Acqua & Sapone team. He was soon riding in Cipo's lead-out train, joining the likes of Guido Trenti, Mario Scirea, and Giovanni Lombardi, helping their leader on the road to many victories.

Over time, Bennati was allowed to sprint for himself and the 2007 and 2008 seasons were his most successful. In 2008, Bennati rode virtually the entire Giro d'Italia in this Maglia Ciclamino points jersey, apart from just two days, battling Mark Cavendish to three stage victories and also taking the Azzurri d'Italia classification.

This busy jersey design, with its many logos, is quintessentially Italian. This is the year that Santini enhanced the jersey's *ciclamino* hue, and as a result the jersey looks brighter than ever.

2008

SERRAMENTI/ PVC DIQUIGIOVANNI/ ANDRONI GIOCATTOLI TEAM JERSEY

Manufacturer: Santini

Associated bike: Guerciotti

Key riders: Daniele Nardello, Michele Scarponi

This Serramenti/Diquigiovanni team jersey continues with the European look of previous designs, featuring a huge variety of sponsors. The team's links with Colombia had been dropped, in favour of a new sponsorship arrangement for 2008 with Venezuela.

It was rumoured that the more diminutive riders actually had one or two of the team's many sponsors missing from their team-issue jerseys due to the super-small size of their upper bodies and the vast number of sponsors!

2008
ASSOS SIX-DAY RACE JERSEY

Manufacturer: Assos

Associated bike: none

Key rider: none

This contemporary jersey was first released by Assos in 2008, one of a number of similar jerseys that have been in the Assos range for a few years.

When first released, the jersey was part of a box set, containing a jersey along with a matching cap, socks, and track mitts. The set came in a very well-presented gift box, which contained a booklet introducing the world of the six-day track race to the masses.

2008
EUSKALTEL/ PAYS BASQUE PRO TEAM JERSEY

Manufacturer: Etxeondo

Associated bike: Orbea

Key riders: Samuel Sánchez, Haimar Zubeldia

When they were riding in France, the Spanish Euskaltel team replaced the usual "Euskadi" logo with "Pays Basque" for the French-speaking audience. While the name change didn't go entirely unnoticed, most fans were simply happy to watch the orange-clad mountain specialists enjoy the high peaks of the Alps and Pyrenees.

This jersey design also included a classy white-fade effect, which was introduced in the 2007 design.

Although Haimar Zubeldia was known for riding silently up the ladder in the overall classification, it was Samuel Sánchez who got the team's biggest win of the year, in the Beijing Olympic road race – albeit in Santini-branded Spanish team kit!

2008

TEAM HIGH ROAD/GIANT/ SRM TEAM JERSEY

Manufacturer: MOA Nalini

Associated bike: Giant

Key riders: Mark Cavendish, George Hincapie

Despite promising performances from riders like Mark Cavendish, Deutsche Telekom lost patience in November 2007 and ended its sponsorship in the peloton. Team owner Bob Stapleton changed the team name, and a sponsorless team kit was hastily put together by MOA.

An all-black kit worn in training for the 2008 season was replaced by this white version when the racing started. The team had a great start to the season, resulting in American company Columbia Sportswear agreeing sponsorship terms in time for the Tour de France (see below).

2008

COLUMBIA/HIGH ROAD/GIANT TEAM JERSEY

Manufacturer: MOA Nalini

Associated bike: Giant

Key riders: Mark Cavendish, Edvald Boasson Hagen

Columbia Sportswear announced their sponsorship of both the men's and women's teams known as Team High Road in July 2008 at the start of the Tour de France.

With the team's name changing again, this time to "Team Columbia", MOA Nalini had to design their third kit of the season. Gone was the clean-looking white and black kit (see above), which was absorbed by the Columbia Sportswear logos and branding palette. It was a worthwhile exercise, however, as Cavendish took four stages in the Tour de France and team mate Marcus Burghardt one, resulting in maximum publicity for the corporate sponsor.

2008
AUSTRALIAN NATIONAL TEAM JERSEY

Manufacturer: Santini
Associated bike: none
Key riders: Cadel Evans, Anna Meares

The Australian National team have consistently produced champions on road, track, BMX, and mountain bike, and Santini have partnered the team for more than ten years.

Due to the complex nature of corporate sponsorship of the Olympic and Commonweath Games, cyclists representing their country in these events often have to wear a different kit to usual, normally with only a single logo from the garment manufacturer appearing on it (see page 130). This jersey is an example of the kit worn year-round when there are fewer restrictions in place.

2008
IRISH CHAMPION JERSEY WITH PEZULA/DOLAN

Manufacturer: Santini
Associated bike: Dolan
Key rider: none

This is a replica of the Irish Champion jersey that Ciarán Power wore in the 2008 season, riding for the small-budget Pezula pro team.

In recent years, Dan Martin, Nicolas Roche, and Matt Brammeier have worn versions of the Irish Champion jersey, all with different numbers of three-leaf clovers on them. Martin's version was mainly green to match his team jersey, but the others were perhaps more attractive, simple white jerseys featuring a green band across the chest with a three-leaf clover on the band and further green and orange detailing on the jersey collar and cuffs.

SOUTH AUSTRALIA.COM/ AIS TEAM JERSEY

Manufacturer: Santini

Associated bike: Bianchi

Key riders: Jack Bobridge, Simon Clarke

This vibrant jersey is the result of a collaboration between the South Australian tourist board and the Australian Institute of Sport (AIS), who created a UCI Continental Team to give some of its talented track endurance riders a chance to race against the top professional riders.

Given that the famous Kangaroo Island is located in South Australia, it's no surprise to see the iconic Australian mammal on the jersey.

Riding a *celeste* Bianchi bike was 19-year-old Jack Bobridge who, later in January 2015, fell agonizingly short of breaking the World Hour Record in Melbourne. In 2011 Bobridge had set a new 4-km (2.49-mile) individual pursuit world record in a time of 4:10.53 at the Australian Championships, beating what many considered to be an unbeatable record held by Chris Boardman.

2008
USA CHAMPION JERSEY WITH ROCK RACING

Manufacturer: Rock & Republic

Associated bike: De Rosa

Key rider: Tyler Hamilton

The Rock Racing team was formed by Michael Ball, the man behind the Rock & Republic fashion brand. The formation of the team kits has been greatly influenced by its fashion connection, with some very outlandish designs which often change multiple times during the season. None of the designs has been easy for fans to purchase for themselves.

During a time trial stage of the Tour of California, Mark Cavendish upset Rock Racing's Mario Cipollini by taking one foot off a pedal as he overtook him. Rumour has it that the younger sprinter was making it clear that he could beat the now-veteran rider using just one leg. Cipollini was not amused!

2008 MILRAM/ COLNAGO "KUH" TOUR OF GERMANY JERSEY

Manufacturer: Santini

Associated bike: Colnago

Key rider: none

This special edition jersey was produced by Santini to celebrate the Tour of Germany passing by the Milram company HQ. Milram make dairy products, hence the cow design (*kuh* in German).

The standard team jersey had a very corporate feel, but this special edition introduces an element of fun to what was a rather safe design. It is interesting to note that when Vermarc took over supplying the team clothing the following year, their jersey design had a definite feel of the Kuh jersey about it.

2008
ITALIAN BEIJING OLYMPICS TEAM JERSEY

Manufacturer: Sportful

Associated bike: none

Key riders: Vincenzo Nibali, Davide Rebellin

Sportful have done a wonderful job of incorporating a little Chinese influence into the national team jersey in honour of the Beijing Olympics. They also changed the predominant background colour of the jersey from blue to white, to try to reflect the heat in Beijing.

The Italian team, which included a young Vincenzo Nibali, rode a strong race with Davide Rebellin taking the silver medal behind the eventual winner, Samuel Sánchez. Sadly, Rebellin's medal was later taken away from him following positive tests for banned substances.

▶ Travelling at speeds in excess of 70km (43.5 miles) per hour in Beijing's Laoshan Velodrome, the Italian track team wore all-in-one skinsuits to save valuable watts in their quest for glory.

UCI WORLD CHAMPION JERSEY WITH LAMPRE/NGC/ WILIER

Manufacturer: Santini
Associated bike: Wilier Triestina
Key rider: Alessandro Ballan

In 2008, Alessandro Ballan followed the now well-trodden path of riding the Vuelta a España as preparation for the World Championships, and he actually won a stage along the way.

During the World Championships, held on an undulating circuit in Varese, Italy, Ballan made a decisive break on the final lap of the race. From a group of 12 he attacked in the closing stages and held off the chasers by a slender margin – a popular home crowd victory for sure!

As Santini are an official supplier to the UCI, they were able to replicate the officially licensed World Champion jersey with the relevant team logos – in this case Lampre, NGC, and Wilier – to make this crisp, clean jersey available to fans.

2008
TIRRENO–ADRIATICO LEADER'S JERSEY

Manufacturer: Santini

Associated bike: none

Key rider: Fabian Cancellara

This jersey is from the 43rd edition of the Tirreno–Adriatico race, which covers 1,122km (697 miles) over seven stages. In 2008, Fabian Cancellara (Team CSC) took the title, an unexpected victory as the race is usually won by climbers.

This shade of blue was new to 2008, replacing the iconic red and yellow jersey. It was a fairly unusual colour in the peloton at the time, so it enabled fans and, crucially, riders to identify the leader of the race more easily. Luckily the colour also works very well with the logo of sponsor EstaTHÉ.

SLIPSTREAM/ CHIPOTLE/H30 TEAM JERSEY

Manufacturer: Pearl Izumi

Associated bike: Felt Bicycles

Key riders: Ryder Hesjedal, David Millar

Cycle jersey design has come a long way in the last 50 years, but many feel that the current pro team jerseys are just a collection of corporate logos confined within strict brand guidelines.

However, in September 2007, the American Slipstream team launched a competition for their fans to design the 2008 team jersey. Team owners Doug Ellis and Jonathan Vaughters were to select the best five designs for the public to vote on, and the only requirement was that the design incorporated the argyle pattern.

The winning jersey features a YKK zip and mesh side panels. But the most interesting element is the printed burrito sticking out of the jersey's rear pocket, which highlights sponsor Chipotle's product without cluttering up the design.

2009
TEAM KATUSHA ITALIAN SPECIAL EDITION JERSEY

Manufacturer: Santini

Associated bike: Ridley

Key rider: Filippo Pozzato

In December 2009, Santini produced a one-off skinsuit for Filippo "Pippo" Pozzato to wear in a charity cycle-cross race, "Move to Improve", which was organized by Tom Boonen and Wilfried Peeters in Mol, Belgium.

The event featured a number of top road riders competing with friendly rivalry on a sandy course, along with an auction and a charity dinner. Pozzato later wore the kit in the 2010 edition of the Paris–Roubaix as a tribute to the late Franco Ballerini.

2009
CRITÉRIUM DU DAUPHINÉ LIBÉRÉ LEADER'S JERSEY

Manufacturer: Santini

Associated bike: none

Key rider: none

This yellow jersey is a replica of the one given to the leaders of the 61st edition of the Critérium du Dauphiné Libéré stage race. Held in the Dauphiné region of France every year, the race serves as a warm-up for the Tour de France, but it is important to remember that it is still the second-biggest race in France and incredibly important in its own right.

The first edition of the race was in 1947 and was sponsored by the local newspaper, the *Dauphiné Libéré*. In 2010 the Amaury Sport Organization (ASO) took over the running of the event, so it is now known simply as the Critérium du Dauphiné.

While there is nothing cutting-edge about this jersey, its pleasant design efficiently incorporates the race name, the sponsor's logo and the all-important colour yellow.

2009
JAN JANSSEN CLASSIC EVENT JERSEY

Manufacturer: Santini

Associated bike: none

Key rider: Jan Janssen

Jan Janssen was the first Dutch rider to win the Tour de France and the Vuelta a España. He was also the World Champion in 1964.

This jersey, which bears the cyclist's image, celebrates an event that takes his name, the Jan Janssen Classic, an annual sportive in which amateurs compete against the clock over various distances.

Santini have adorned the jersey with the names of the famous bergs (hills) that the riders will encounter in this event, making it a fitting memento for anybody finishing the full 200km (124 miles) of the event.

2009
ITALIAN CHAMPION JERSEY WITH KATUSHA

Manufacturer: Santini
Associated bike: Ridley
Key rider: Filippo Pozzato

Filippo "Pippo" Pozzato rode with Katusha for the 2009–11 seasons. Without doubt the highlight of a stellar 2009 season was his win in the Italian National Championships.

Pozzato was presented with a standard Maglia Tricolore on the podium, but he went through three different jersey designs before finally settling on this one as both of the earlier designs fell foul of the Italian racing authorities.

All was forgotten by the fans when Pozzato won Stage 12 of the 2010 Giro d'Italia, with his hands aloft in the National Champion jersey.

2009
CERVÉLO TESTTEAM/ZIPP/ CASTELLI/ZIPVIT AERO JERSEY

Manufacturer: Castelli
Associated bike: Cervélo
Key riders: Thor Hushovd, Carlos Sastre

Cervélo TestTeam's black 2009 team kit raised concerns of overheating so, in late June of that year, Castelli released a white version to provide relief from the heat of the Tour de France. The white kit had an improved aero design that would save 10 watts at 40km (25 miles) per hour, giving a 40-second advantage over the course of 40km (25 miles).

A focus group of Cervélo TestTeam riders worked with Castelli clothing engineers to improve kit for cold and wet conditions. Castelli developed a stretchy, short-sleeved rain jersey to wear with water-resistant Nanoflex arm warmers in the foul weather of the spring classics.

2009
GIRO D'ITALIA
CENTOANNI
OVERALL
LEADER'S
JERSEY

Manufacturer: Santini

Associated bike: none

Key rider: none

This Maglia Rosa was designed by the famous Italian fashion duo Dolce & Gabbana to celebrate the 100th anniversary of the very first Giro d'Italia.

The jersey design features plenty of tricolore references but, sadly, the Dolce & Gabbana logo on the collar did not appear on the replica jerseys which were available for fans to buy at the race or online.

Of course, the 100th anniversary (*Centoanni*) race was actually only the 92nd edition of the Giro d'Italia, as the two world wars interrupted the running of the race.

THE
PRESENT DAY

||||||||||||||||||||||||||||||||||||||||||||||||||||||||||||||||||||||||||||||||||||||||||||

Compared with the key improvements in cycle clothing over time, the changes that have come about in recent years have been "marginal gains", a phrase coined by Sir David Brailsford.

However, Castelli did make a giant leap forward in their unique relationship with the Cervélo TestTeam, making the most of their association with the team by using the riders to help them in the development of their garments. Professional rider Gabriel Rasch (nicknamed Gabba) came up with the idea of a stretchy, form-fitting short-sleeved rain jersey designed for the foul weather of the spring classics, improving on the hard-shell jackets in use.

The Gabba jersey was gradually developed, an all-weather soft-shell aerodynamic garment made from water-repellent fabrics which shed water without the heat build-up. Soon many of the pro teams were buying Gabba jerseys and peeling off Castelli's trademark scorpion logo to keep their sponsors happy.

Another slower-burning development has been in the concept of the aero jersey. This chapter features many aero jerseys, produced by a range of manufacturers all with the same aim: using textured fabrics to make the air flow over the rider as efficiently as possible, without compromising the fit and comfort of the garment.

◀ Sir Bradley Wiggins (Team Sky) took the overall win in the 2011 Critérium du Dauphiné. While Team Sky are sponsored by Adidas, the race leaders' jerseys are sponsored by Santini. Cycling must be one of the only sports where two competing apparel brands appear on one garment.

2010
TEAM SKY/
ADIDAS TEAM
JERSEY

Manufacturer: Adidas

Associated bike: Pinarello

Key riders: Bradley Wiggins,
Geraint Thomas

After a stint sponsoring the GB track team, BSkyB stepped up their involvement in cycling to be the title sponsor for a brand-new British professional team. They initially released the names of six British riders who would be on the team (Thomas, Cummings, Froome, Downing, Stannard, and Kennaugh), but it was the eagerly anticipated signing of Bradley Wiggins from Garmin/Slipstream that gave the team abundant media publicity before they'd even turned a pedal.

Their goal was to create the first-ever British Tour de France winner, which they achieved with Bradley Wiggins just two years later in 2012.

The team's identity was designed by London agency Antidote, who developed "The Line", a philosophy they applied to the kit, bikes, vehicles, website and merchandise.

ANDRONI GIOCATTOLI/ SERRAMENTI/ PVC DIQUIGIOVANNI TEAM JERSEY

Manufacturer: Santini

Associated bike: Guerciotti

Key riders: Michele Scarponi, José Serpa

T he Androni team had two versions of their jersey for 2010. This was the first, but when Sidermec came on board as a replacement sponsor for Sittam, their logo was added at the bottom of the jersey and the second version was worn later in the season.

The team rode Guerciotti bicycles, but there is no sign of the Guerciotti logo on the team's jersey. The bike brand sponsored the team from 2007 until the 2010 season, with Bianchi taking over in 2011.

VACANSOLEIL/ BATAVUS/ COLLSTROP/BBB TEAM JERSEY

Manufacturer: Santini

Associated bike: Batavus

Key riders: Johnny Hoogerland, Wout Poels

The Vacansoleil/Batavus/ Collstrop/BBB team put in a good performance in the Tour of Britain in 2010, with Borut Božič winning a stage and finishing second overall, Johnny Hoogerland winning the mountains classification, and the team being named as winners in the overall category.

Santini have made an elegant design out of the Vacansoleil logos, giving the team a cheerful and dramatic jersey in the peloton.

Rather than his racing results, Johnny Hoogerland is probably best known for a terrible accident that took place in the following year's Tour de France. He was hit by a media car, causing him to crash into a barbed wire fence.

2010
GF FELICE GIMONDI CELEBRATION JERSEY

Manufacturer: Santini

Associated bike: Bianchi

Key rider: Felice Gimondi

This elaborate jersey was made for the amateur cyclists taking part in the 2010 Granfondo Felice Gimondi. It was designed by Santini to celebrate the different team and leaders' jerseys that the great Felice Gimondi wore during his career.

The jersey made for the tenth edition of the race was a much simpler design with a white background and a multi-coloured peloton, but this fifteenth edition jersey has a lot more detail, with a silhouette of Gimondi himself used for the outline.

2010

TOUR DOWN UNDER OVERALL LEADER'S JERSEY

Manufacturer: Santini

Associated bike: none

Key rider: André Greipel

André Greipel won the first stage in the 2010 Tour Down Under, then continued to wear this stylish overall leader's jersey right until the end of the race, holding off Spain's Luis León Sánchez.

The 2010 TDU actually awarded six jerseys on the podium at the end of each stage, but due to UCI rules only four (overall, mountains, points, and young rider) could be worn during the race. The remaining two (best team and most aggressive rider) were presented on the podium, but the winners wore their regular team jerseys the following day.

2010

XACOBEO GALICIA/BH TEAM JERSEY

Manufacturer: Etxeondo

Associated bike: BH Bikes

Key rider: Ezequiel Mosquera

Following the success of the Basque regional government's sponsorship of the Euskaltel-Euskadi team, the Galician regional government decided to sponsor Xacobeo Galicia/BH.

It's odd that the team ended up with the same clothing manufacturer too. Etxeondo supplied them for the 2009 and 2010 seasons, with a striking design of oblique lines across the bottom of the jersey.

Xacobeo Galicia received wildcard invitations to the Vuelta a España, with three stage wins to their credit over the years.

2010
VENEZUELAN NATIONAL TEAM JERSEY

Manufacturer: Santini

Associated bike: none

Key rider: Jackson Rodríguez

Santini made this jersey for the two riders selected for the Venezuelan National Team, taking part in the 2010 World Championships in Geelong, Melbourne, Australia. They certainly stood out in the peloton with this striking design, which mirrors the colours and stars of the national flag.

The inevitable early break went before the race even left Melbourne, and it contained Jackson Rodríguez of Venezuela as well as four other riders. They gained over 23 minutes at one point, so plenty of fans got to appreciate this colourful kit.

2010
LAMPRE/ FARNESE VINI/ WILIER/GEOX BLACK EDITION TEAM JERSEY

Manufacturer: Santini

Associated bike: Wilier Triestina

Key rider: Gilberto Simoni

This fabulous special edition jersey was designed to celebrate Gilberto Simoni's final ride in the Giro d'Italia, after starting out as a professional in 1994 for the Jolly Componibili/Cage team.

The basic design was inspired by the standard Lampre kit, but the black background was added to make it wildly different. It was intended to look like he had a formal suit on at the end of the stage. The contrasting pink stitching was a nod to the team's traditional jersey colour.

2010
VUELTA A COLOMBIA 60TH ANNIVERSARY JERSEY

Manufacturer: Suarez

Associated bike: none

Key riders: Luis Herrera, Fabio Parra

Suarez produced this colourful, patriotic jersey to celebrate the 60th anniversary of the start of the extraordinarily tough Vuelta a Colombia national tour.

The organizers assembled many former winners for a photograph before the start of the race, including greats like Luis Herrera, Oliverio Rincón, Fabio Parra, and Chepe González. In fact, even the 1951 winner, Efraín Forero Triviño, was present!

2010
MAPEI DAY CELEBRATION JERSEY

Manufacturer: Santini

Associated bike: none

Key rider: Franco Ballerini

This celebration jersey was made by event sponsor Santini for the 2010 Mapei Day, a fantastic annual multi-sport event which takes place in July in Italy. The stunning graphic design of this jersey was created in memory of Franco Ballerini, a former Mapei professional who sadly died in a car rally at Larciano in 2010.

All of the Mapei celebration jerseys feature a cheerful and often eccentric design. The 2010 edition is no exception, yet for once it doesn't depict an animal that is native to the area. Santini produce a jersey for the event every year, and other designs have featured animals such as eagles, ibexes, and foxes.

2010
DELOITTE RIDE ACROSS BRITAIN JERSEY

Manufacturer: Adidas

Associated bike: none

Key riders: Dame Sarah Storey, Barney Storey MBE

The Deloitte Ride Across Britain (RAB) 2010 was launched on 24 July 2009 and, by 13 August, all the places were taken. The ride raised over £380,000 for ParalympicsGB to help fund the athletes that were training for and taking part in the London 2012 Olympics.

Going from Land's End to John O'Groats, the RAB takes place over nine days, the riders averaging 174km (108 miles) per day.

This simple and corporate design from Adidas was worn by a number of TeamGB's paralympic cyclists as well as members of the public.

2010
TOUR DE FRANCE OVERALL LEADER'S JERSEY WITH SAXO BANK

Manufacturer: Nike

Associated bike: Specialized

Key rider: Fabian Cancellara

After winning the 8.9-km (5½-mile) Prologue in Rotterdam, Fabian Cancellara went on to wear the race leader's Maillot Jaune, beating Tony Martin and David Millar with a time of exactly ten minutes.

Unlike the Discovery Channel version, this jersey was never available for the general public to buy. This is because the leader's jersey is made by Nike but the team's technical clothing sponsor is Sportful. These two competing brands could not be present on the same garment in the retail market.

2010
GB NATIONAL TEAM JERSEY WITH SKY/ HALFORDS

Manufacturer: Adidas

Associated bike: Trek

Key riders: Sir Chris Hoy, Sir Bradley Wiggins

This powerful design was created for British Cycling by sportswear giant Adidas, but made in Italy by MOA Nalini. The basic look of the kit had been developed in 2006 and remained unchanged for seven years, with sponsors Halfords, BikeHut, Sky, and Gatorade coming and going and helping to create a phenomenal 52 World Champions over the different events.

Incredibly, such is the power of sponsors over governing bodies, in 2009 the words "Great Britain" were actually dropped from the design in favour of additional sponsor logos.

In January 2013, a joint press release from Adidas and British Cycling announced a radically different new jersey design for the 2013/2014 seasons (see page 203).

2010
GIRO D'ITALIA BLACK FAUSTO COPPI WOOL JERSEY

Manufacturer: Santini

Associated bike: none

Key rider: Fausto Coppi

Although the pink jersey made by Santini to celebrate the 70th anniversary of Fausto Coppi's first Maglia Rosa (see opposite) was limited to a production run of 500, only 200 of this special edition black version were made. This is a subtler affair, allowing the more discerning Giro fan to show allegiance to the Italian Tour without dressing head-to-toe in pink.

It's a great-looking jersey, which I have actually worn more often off the bike than on it!

GIRO D'ITALIA PINK FAUSTO COPPI WOOL JERSEY

Manufacturer: Santini

Associated bike: Bianchi

Key rider: Fausto Coppi

In conjunction with the organizers of the Giro d'Italia, Santini produced this incredible jersey, made in Italy of the very finest wool, to celebrate the 70th anniversary of Fausto Coppi's first overall leader's pink jersey.

Made with a 50 per cent wool and 50 per cent acrylic mix, this jersey is easier to care for than an all-wool equivalent. Other nice design touches include the old-school embroidered badges, Santini-branded metal buttons on the rear pockets, a retro metal zipper, embroidered lettering on the chest, and the all-important limited edition numbered label (this example is number 125 out of 500).

2010
GIRO D'ITALIA MAGLIA NERA FASHION JERSEY

Manufacturer: Santini

Associated bike: none

Key rider: none

Thanks to their sponsorship of the Giro d'Italia, every year Santini produce a fashion range to complement the leaders' jerseys for the year. This jersey, from the 2010 collection, features a bold contrast between black and pink, and attractive elasticated Italian tricolore sleeve cuffs.

Although many cycling purists now look down on the wearing of leaders' jerseys, examples like this do allow fans, whether on the bike or off, to show their appreciation of what is a very exciting annual tour.

2011
TOUR OF THE BASQUE COUNTRY OVERALL LEADER'S JERSEY

Manufacturer: Etxeondo

Associated bike: none

Key rider: Samuel Sánchez

The Tour of the Basque Country (Vuelta Ciclista al País Vasco) is one of my favourite stage races in the annual cycling calendar. Other races may have bigger budgets, greater social media, and more extensive television coverage, yet the Tour of the Basque Country always makes for fantastic viewing.

The leaders' jerseys are supplied by Etxeondo, who are located in Irura in the Basque Country. Many of the jersey sponsors are local to the region, so their logos have supporting Basque text and always have a great look about them.

WORLD CHAMPION JERSEY WITH HORIZON FITNESS

Manufacturer: Santini

Associated bike: Dolan

Key rider: Dame Sarah Storey

It's not often you get to be involved in creating the clothing for a genuine World Champion, and it's even rarer when it is a member of your family! This jersey was designed for Dame Sarah Storey (my sister-in-law) for the 2011 season after she won the Paracycling World Championships.

There are many rules and regulations associated with creating a UCI World Champion jersey. Only a very limited number of logos is allowed and the size of every logo is tightly controlled to ensure that the jersey design is respected.

I did end up with a jersey in my size, and it is a nice memento from the 2011 season.

GIANNI BUGNO SPECIAL EDITION WORLD CHAMPION JERSEY

Manufacturer: Santini

Associated bike: none

Key rider: Gianni Bugno

Launched in the summer of 2011, this limited edition wool jersey was designed by Santini to celebrate the 20th anniversary of Gianni Bugno's wins at the Road World Championships in Stuttgart in 1991 and Benidorm in 1992.

With only 1,000 made, each jersey was individually numbered (this is jersey number 555) and featured Bugno's signature embroidered on the chest, Santini-branded metal buttons, and an authentic-looking metal zip, all packaged in an elegant tin with a retro image of Bugno himself.

Happily, Bugno was present at Santini's annual party at the Eurobike show to help publicize the launch of the product.

2011
TIRRENO–ADRIATICO OVERALL LEADER'S JERSEY

Manufacturer: Santini

Associated bike: none

Key rider: Cadel Evans

Cadel Evans (BMC team) took the 2011 edition of the Tirreno–Adriatico, holding off Dutch climber Robert Gesink. Fabian Cancellara won the time trial, happy to take his first-ever victory in Leopard/Trek kit.

The Tirreno–Adriatico leaders' jerseys very much adopted the look of the Giro d'Italia leaders' jerseys in 2011, with the contrasting piping, mesh side panels, and the tricolore rising from the bottom hem.

Italian road racing cyclist Franco Ballerini's name appeared on the collar of all leaders' jerseys in 2011 to commemorate his life on the bike.

2011
MOLDOVAN CHAMPION JERSEY WITH KATUSHA/ GAZPROM

Manufacturer: Santini

Associated bike: Focus

Key rider: none

Alexandre Pliuşchin has won his National Road Championship four times, as well as representing Moldova in the 2008 Olympic Games in Beijing, in both the road race and the individual pursuit. Pliuşchin also won the Duo Normand, a two-man time trial, with Artem Ovechkin in 2010. The event is held every September in Normandy, France, and is popular with club racers from the UK. I rode it myself in 1999 with a friend, yet despite our best efforts we were overtaken by Chris Boardman and Jen Voigt on their way to victory!

This unique jersey is rarely seen in the European peloton so it's a delight to have it in my collection.

2011
CRITÉRIUM DU DAUPHINÉ OVERALL LEADER'S JERSEY

Manufacturer: Santini
Associated bike: none
Key rider: Bradley Wiggins

The Critérium leader's jersey is exactly the same colour as that for the Tour de France, and there is very little difference in the design, with only the sponsors' logos changing from year to year.

The 2011 edition of the race was won by Bradley Wiggins (Team Sky) who took the lead after a strong time trial stage and maintained his advantage to the end of the race – a tactic that has proved fruitful in other races too.

But Wiggins was not the first Briton to win the Critérium; earlier wins went to the pioneer Brian Robinson, who took the race in 1961, and Robert Millar after him in 1990.

CRITÉRIUM DU DAUPHINÉ KING OF THE MOUNTAINS JERSEY WITH KATUSHA

Manufacturer: Santini
Associated bike: none
Key rider: Joaquim Rodríguez

The Dauphiné polka-dot jersey is one of the few mountain leaders' jerseys with white spots on a red background, as opposed to the more traditional red spots on white.

This jersey was created by Santini for replica sales, and is identical to the design that Rodríguez would have worn, just available in much bigger sizes. At only 57kg (125lb), Rodríguez is rather smaller than most amateur riders.

2011
CRITÉRIUM DU DAUPHINÉ POINTS JERSEY WITH KATUSHA

Manufacturer: Santini

Associated bike: none

Key rider: Joaquim Rodríguez

During the Tour de France, cycling fans are used to seeing sprinters like Erik Zabel, Mark Cavendish, Peter Sagan, and André Greipel vying for the green points jersey in the intermediate and bunch sprints. But during the 2011 Critérium, Joaquim Rodríguez unusually won both the King of the Mountains and the points classification.

The Tour de France typically allocates a greater number of points for flatter stages, but other stage races often opt to do something a little different to keep the fans interested. Seeing Rodríguez in a mountain leader's jersey is not unusual, as he is known for his skill as a climber, but seeing him in a green points jersey is.

2011
EUSKALTEL/ EUSKADI PRO TEAM JERSEY

Manufacturer: MOA Nalini

Associated bike: Orbea

Key riders: Samuel Sánchez, Igor Antón

The bright orange flash of the Euskaltel/Euskadi team often lights up the mountain stages, with the likes of 2008 Olympic Champion Samuel Sánchez, Igor Antón, and Amets Txurruka enjoying life on tough gradients.

MOA took over from Etxeondo as technical partner to the team in 2009, supplying the team kit until 2012. MOA continued with the basic design that Etxeondo had pioneered over the years, as it was still a strong look and one that Basque fans were happy to wear with great pride.

2011
LEOPARD/ TREK PRO TEAM JERSEY

Manufacturer: Craft

Associated bike: Trek

Key riders: Andy Schleck, Jens Voigt

Many modern professional cycling teams have up to 30 sponsors, each wanting their logo in a prominent position on the team's clothing to get some return for their often considerable investment. As a result, modern pro team jerseys are often a touch messy, with designers having to accommodate countless logos and follow numerous corporate guidelines.

Using just three colours and a minimal number of logos, the design of this 2011 aero jersey was seen by many as the correct way to do it – a step back in time to the old and iconic retro wool jerseys, when teams had fewer sponsors to keep happy.

2011
LUXEMBOURG CHAMPION JERSEY WITH LEOPARD/TREK

Manufacturer: Craft
Associated bike: Trek
Key rider: Frank Schleck

Based on the cool and uncomplicated design of the team's standard jersey (see opposite), the Luxembourg Champion aero jersey was destined to have the same simple feel.

The Leopard/Trek identity was designed by the Minale Design Strategy agency, who ensured that all branding looked consistent, from the team's website and team bus to the rider's bikes and clothing.

ANDRONI GIOCATTOLI PRO TEAM JERSEY

Manufacturer: Santini

Associated bike: Bianchi

Key riders: Emanuele Sella, Roberto Ferrari

This kit wins the award for the most sponsors per square centimetre of jersey. The best you can say about this jersey is that its numerous logos make the design look unquestionably European.

This colourful, logo-heavy design has stayed similar for a number of years, keeping the team afloat on the backs of a variety of smaller sponsors – an achievement of which team manager Gianni Savio is very proud, and rightly so.

2011
GIRO D'ITALIA OVERALL LEADER'S PRO JERSEY

Manufacturer: Santini

Associated bike: Specialized

Key rider: Alberto Contador

Alberto Contador won the 2011 edition of the Giro, but a positive drugs test in 2010 for Clenbuterol led, in 2012, to a two-year ban and the wiping of his name from the results.

The Saxo Bank logo really sets off this fabulous jersey. The design celebrates the 150th anniversary of Italian unification, symbolized by the number and tricolore line under the sponsor panel.

Having two competing clothing brands on the sponsor panel (Santini, who were the race sponsors, and Sportful, who were the team sponsors) presented insurmountable problems with the complex contractual licensing agreements for replica sales, so this jersey was never available for retail sales. It was made only as a gift for team staff and sponsors.

2011
RAPHA/ CONDOR/SHARP TEAM JERSEY

Manufacturer: Rapha

Associated bike: Condor

Key riders: Kristian House, Ed Clancy

C lothing manufacturer Rapha was almost inextricably linked to this team until the end of 2014. During their nine-year involvement, experienced team manager John Herety built a squad that took national titles, dominated UK racing, and achieved success abroad, as well as allowing its young racers to move to bigger teams.

To commemorate their time with the team, Rapha produced a small number of tasteful, special edition jerseys and T-shirts with specially commissioned graphics and embroidery.

Mavic took over the clothing sponsorship in 2015, adding flashes of yellow (their corporate colour) to the kit as well as supplying shoes and helmets.

2011
RAPHA/ CONDOR/JLT TEAM LONDON NOCTURNE JERSEY

Manufacturer: Rapha

Associated bike: Condor

Key riders: Graham Briggs, Ed Clancy

Dubbed the "Men in Black" during the popular televised Tour Series circuit races, in front of 10,000 fans at London's Smithfield Meat Market the Rapha/Condor/JLT riders became the men in white for the IG Markets Smithfield Nocturne.

That night they rode in one-off white speed-suits, which had been designed for the occasion by Sir Paul Smith. The special edition kit was developed to raise money for the Japanese earthquake appeal. The jersey design was showcased for one night only at the Smithfield Nocturne and the 150 special edition jerseys, available for the public to buy online, sold out in 20 minutes.

2011
TOUR DE FRANCE LEADER'S JERSEY WITH GARMIN/ CERVÉLO

Manufacturer: Nike

Associated bike: Cervélo

Key rider: Thor Hushovd

Many riders complain of the curse of the rainbow jersey, but Thor Hushovd's remarkable performance during the 2011 Tour de France threw this curse into question. Hushovd first claimed the yellow in Stage 2, when his Garmin/Cervélo team won the time trial. He kept it for a week, with Cadel Evans biting at his heels.

After his stint in the yellow jersey, Hushovd went on the attack during Stage 13. He was one of the first over the Col d'Aubisque, then used his super-fast descending skills to pass the leaders and take the victory.

Those skills were again displayed in Stage 16 when he was among those who went clear on the Col de Manse before he took the final sprint to take his second stage of the tour.

▶ World Champion Thor Hushovd (Garmin) enjoys the extra room and respect offered by his fellow competitors due to his wearing the yellow jersey.

2012
TOUR DOWN UNDER OVERALL LEADER'S JERSEY

Manufacturer: Santini

Associated bike: Colnago

Key rider: Simon Gerrans

The 14th edition of the Tour Down Under was won by Simon Gerrans (GreenEDGE) after he took the lead on the penultimate stage.

While several races have a yellow leader's jersey, for many fans the colour is primarily associated with the Tour de France and, to a lesser extent, the Paris–Nice and Critérium du Dauphiné races. So having an ochre-coloured jersey for the leader of the TDU distinguishes this race.

2012
GREENEDGE/ SCOTT TEAM JERSEY

Manufacturer: Santini

Associated bike: Scott

Key riders: Matthew Goss, Simon Gerrans

This aero jersey was released for the newly formed GreenEDGE team just after the Tour Down Under. Taking a design lead from the 2011 Leopard/Trek jersey (see page 184), the design team at Santini produced this clean, elegant kit which went on to win Milan–San Remo thanks to Simon Gerrans.

Later in the 2012 season, Orica signed up as headline sponsor and the team created a new jersey (see page 194).

MATRIX FITNESS/ PRENDAS CICLISMO/ VELOCITE TEAM JERSEY

Manufacturer: Santini

Associated bike: Velocite

Key riders: Annie Simpson, Jo Rowsell

Although Dani King and Jo Rowsell were the big names on the team in 2012, the rider that got the most television coverage was Annie Simpson, who won the UK's annual Johnson Health Tech Grand Prix Series. Simpson won the opening round in Oxford, and continued to ride well to take the overall win.

This jersey looked good both on the riders and on the TV during post-race interviews. Logo placement is important for sponsors and getting their own way during the design process is not always easy. However, getting some television time makes it all worthwhile!

2012
ORICA/ GREENEDGE TEAM JERSEY

Manufacturer: Santini

Associated bike: Scott

Key riders: Matthew Goss, Simon Gerrans

This was the debut year for the GreenEDGE team (see page 192) and by July they had found the main sponsor the team badly needed to maintain its place in the peloton.

Orica were announced as the title sponsor just before the Tour de France (for maximum media exposure), so Santini had to produce a third version of the team kit.

It would appear that the team were happy with the design of this aero jersey, as it has remained fairly constant for some time, despite the change of clothing supplier from Santini to Craft.

2012
SCOTTISH NATIONAL CHAMPION JERSEY WITH RAPHA/CONDOR

Manufacturer: Rapha
Associated bike: Condor
Key rider: James McCallum

Although the Rapha team are generally know as the "Men in Black", this Scottish Champion jersey made for James McCallum has a navy background, which is actually more pleasing on the eye. Rapha sensibly dropped the pink flashes on this champion jersey, keeping it simple with just white logos and details.

McCallum won the Scottish Road Race Championships in 2012, sprinting to victory ahead of his breakaway rival Evan Oliphant in the sprint for the line. McCallum now works as a Sports Director for ONE Pro Cycling.

WORLD CHAMPION JERSEY WITH RAPHA/CONDOR

Manufacturer: Rapha

Associated bike: Condor

Key rider: Andy Tennant

Andy Tennant has been awarded a number of World Track Champion jerseys in his time, the first in 2005 when he won the Junior title. This jersey was awarded when he won the World Track Championships in 2012. Because he was a Track Champion, as opposed to a Road Champion, there is a curve in the centre of the rainbow bands.

The design of this jersey would have been submitted to the UCI for approval before production. They are very protective of their mark and the use of the rainbow bands, right down to the exact colours used.

Santini is the official technical supplier to the UCI, therefore this garment would not have been sold to the public, but was only made for the rider himself.

2013
BLANCO/GIANT TEAM JERSEY

Manufacturer: Etxeondo

Associated bike: Giant

Key rider: Luis León Sánchez

Following a series of scandals in the cycling world, the Rabobank Group announced that they would end their sponsorship of the men's team. As part of the separation deal, they guaranteed to fund the team for the 2013 season. So team manager Richard Plugge decided to start the season riding under the un-sponsored name "Blanco", very much like Team High Road had done previously (see page 147).

The Etxeondo-made Blanco kit was used only until June, after which the team landed Belkin as a title sponsor for the remainder of the season.

This exact jersey was made for Luis León Sánchez, and has his name and the Spanish flag on the mesh side panels to help fans recognize him.

2013
GIRO D'ITALIA OVERALL LEADER'S JERSEY

Manufacturer: Santini

Associated bike: none

Key rider: none

Following on from the typically Italian Maglia Rosa designed by Dolce & Gabbana in 2009 (see page 161), Sir Paul Smith took a more minimalist approach in 2013 when asked to design his take on the iconic leaders' jerseys. Over the years, extra logos, panels, and details had been added, but Sir Paul stripped back the design to the bare essentials, resulting in a much more elegant version for the 2013 edition of the race.

Small touches were added, like the typical colourful sleeve cuff and Sir Paul's own cartoon rider. He also chose a deeper colour of pink.

Sir Paul is a life-long cycling fan, as well as an avid collector of cycling jerseys, so he must have been honoured to be asked to put his mark on the Maglia Rosa.

2013
COCA-COLA JERSEY

Manufacturer: *Santini*

Associated bike: none

Key rider: none

When Santini released photographs of these jerseys leaving their factory bound for Japan, I decided I had to get hold of one. By contacting a friend who lives in Japan, I managed to purchase a jersey and matching shorts.

With a crisp white background and the classic Coca-Cola red, this fantastic jersey looks suitably chic and stylish.

2013
RADIOSHACK/ NISSAN/TREK PRO TEAM JERSEY

Manufacturer: Craft

Associated bike: Trek

Key riders: Fabian Cancellara, Chris Horner

Despite the tremendous success of the Leopard/Trek 2011 clothing design, the team's merger with RadioShack resulted in an awful team kit for 2012. With the inevitable yellow LiveSTRONG band, the 2012 clothing could never live up to the clean, classic design of 2011.

This 2013 version, however, was a vast improvement. This jersey is the Elite Aero version, a super-tight garment for maximum gains in aerodynamics, achieved by using a combination of five different fabrics in the jersey's construction.

2013
KATUSHA/ GAZPROM/ ITERA/CANYON PRO TEAM JERSEY

Manufacturer: Santini

Associated bike: Canyon

Key rider: Joaquim Rodríguez

Santini adapted this aero jersey from their high-tech aerodynamic speed-suit which was created to enhance a rider's performance. To make the professional kit easier for the amateur to use, they produced separate jerseys and bib shorts, which could be connected by an internal zip.

This is a really smart solution, offering all the benefits of a speed-suit while maintaining the comfort and practicality of having two separate garments.

2013
VINI FANTINI/ SELLE ITALIA/ CIPOLLINI PRO TEAM JERSEY

Manufacturer: Giordana

Associated bike: Cipollini

Key riders: Danilo di Luca, Matteo Rabottini

Entering the 2013 Giro d'Italia on the back of a strong team of exciting riders, it seemed as though this eye-catching jersey was going to be one to watch.

Unfortunately, the huge scandal involving Danilo di Luca and Mauro Santambrogio erupted and soon put paid to that, but it's worth noting that Giordana actually created a fabulous technical jersey with this design. It boasts all the modern features that pro riders consider to be essential, but also fits the amateur rider well – not something that many other manufacturers achieve.

2013
SYNERGY/ BAKU CYCLING PROJECT TEAM JERSEY

Manufacturer: Santini

Associated bike: BH Bikes

Key riders: David McCann, Dan Craven

The Synergy/Baku Cycling Project is a UCI Continental team based in Azerbaijan that is run and managed by David McQuaid, rider David McCann, and former Team Sky pro Jeremy Hunt.

This team is funded by both industry names and the national government, who are hoping to develop an Azerbaijani rider to qualify for future Olympic Games.

This dramatic yet quirky design is actually one of the better modern jersey designs of the peloton. It just goes to show that you don't have to be one of the biggest teams to have one of the sharpest jerseys.

2013
UCI WORLD ROAD CHAMPION JERSEY

Manufacturer: Santini

Associated bike: Giant

Key rider: Marianne Vos

Although it's commonly referred to as the rainbow jersey, the World Champion jersey actually only features five bands: blue, red, black, yellow, and green. The five colours represent the five continents, as do the IOC's Olympic rings.

This particular jersey has been signed by Marianne Vos, who is without doubt one of the best cyclists in the world!

2013
GB NATIONAL TEAM JERSEY WITH SKY

Manufacturer: Adidas

Associated bike: Pinarello

Key riders: Laura Trott, Dame Sarah Storey

British Cycling launched this new cycling kit design for the 2013/2014 season. Although there are plenty of Sky logos, once again there is no prominent mention of the country that the riders represent.

Adidas did not supply the clothing for Team Sky in 2013 (Rapha landed the contract), so they concentrated on the national squad, producing both a replica version and a team-issue "AdiStar" jersey.

BELKIN/GIANT/ ETXEONDO TEAM JERSEY

Manufacturer: Etxeondo

Associated bike: Giant

Key rider: Maarten Tjallingii

Recent developments in cycle garment manufacture have all centred around the introduction and improvement of aero clothing for the pro team riders, and this is a great example.

This exact jersey was made for Maarten Tjallingii, a spring classics specialist. At 1.88m (6ft 2in) tall and weighing 77kg (169lb) he is one of the bigger riders in the team, and the jersey features a cloth label marked with his name and printed XL. At the other end of the scale is Bauke Mollema who, despite being 1.81m (5ft 11in) tall, weighs only 64kg (141lb)!

These aero jerseys are made by Etxeondo and have "Giant Powered by Etxeondo" cloth labels. The zips are customized YKK Giant zips, but it is interesting to note that the team's training and winter garments have Etxeondo zip pullers.

2013
RABOBANK–LIV TEAM JERSEY

Manufacturer: Etxeondo

Associated bike: Giant

Key riders: Marianne Vos, Pauline Ferrand-Prévot

This team-issue, female-specific aero jersey is given to the pro riders of the Rabobank/Liv Women's team. Rabobank dropped out of the sponsorship of the men's team in 2012 (due to one too many doping scandals), but they were only too happy to continue sponsoring the women's team. The team ride Giant bicycles through its female-specific brand Liv.

Riding for the team, Marianne Vos is arguably one of the most complete riders the world has ever seen, able to win on the road, track, cyclo-cross, and mountain bike. She certainly deserves the comparison to Eddy Merckx. However, Pauline Ferrand-Prévot has recently taken the team leader position, largely thanks to her being a reigning four-time world champion at road, cyclo-cross, mountain bike cross country, and team relay.

2014
ROCKET ESPRESSO MILANO JERSEY

Manufacturer: Santini

Associated bike: none

Key rider: none

There is an affinity between cyclists and coffee, and this is evident in the growth of cycling café culture.

This popular jersey was designed for the same company by Santini's lead designer Fergus Niland for Prendas Ciclismo. A worthy donation is made to the Dave Rayner Fund for every garment sold. The fund was set up after the tragic death of English professional racing cyclist Dave Rayner, to remember him by giving other young riders the chance to follow in Dave's footsteps by gaining valuable experience in European teams.

2014
CINELLI/SANTINI TEAM JERSEY

Manufacturer: Santini

Associated bike: Cinelli

Key rider: Olga Cappiello

It's ironic that Cinelli and Santini – two pillars of Italian cycling – are brought together by way of an amateur Granfondo cycling team, as opposed to a high-profile professional team.

The prominent Cinelli logo was redesigned in 1979 when company president Antonio Colombo asked designer Italo Lupi to come up with a new look. Lupi created one of the most imitated logos in the peloton.

The colours of the winged C had nothing to do with cycling; they were inspired by the enamelling on old British locomotives, and Lupi simply chose them because he thought they looked chic.

2014
WANTY/GROUPE GOBERT/GSG/ KUOTA TEAM JERSEY

Manufacturer: Giessegi

Associated bike: Kuota

Key rider: Björn Leukemans

Previously known as Accent Jobs/ Wanty in 2013, this team is typical among Belgian teams on the UCI Pro Continental circuit, with its riders performing well in the spring classics.

The team jersey is highly visible in the peloton, mainly due to the block of blue being used for both the jersey and shorts.

Team clothing sponsor Giessegi (GSG) is an Italian company with a good heritage in the clothing business who recently celebrated their 30th anniversary. The company was founded in 1984 by Simone Fraccaro, a professional rider from 1974 to 1984, who would have actually worn the GIS Gelati/Olmo wool jersey featured on page 32.

2014
WELSH COMMONWEALTH GAMES TEAM JERSEY

Manufacturer: Craft
Associated bike: none
Key rider: Geraint Thomas

This jersey is exactly the same specification as those supplied to the Welsh riders for the 2014 Commonwealth Games, a super-tight garment created to achieve maximum gains in aerodynamics. This type of aero jersey looked great on the team riders, and resulted in a gold medal for Wales thanks to Geraint Thomas.

It was an epic ride by Thomas, who broke away from the chasers with just 14km (8½ miles) remaining. The weather proved too much for most of the peloton and only 14 of the 139 riders finished the race in the horrendously wet conditions.

2014
ENJOY COCA-COLA JERSEY

Manufacturer: Santini

Associated bike: none

Key rider: none

V ery similar in construction to the previous version (see page 199), this jersey opts for a slightly different, more colourful design approach as well as one or two physical tweaks.

One small but important addition is the covered zip. A full zip is essential to provide extra ventilation in the heat, but covering the zip allows the design of the jersey to be maintained uninterrupted across the chest.

2014
MOVISTAR/ CANYON/ ENDURA PRO TEAM JERSEY

Manufacturer: Endura

Associated bike: Canyon

Key riders: Alex Dowsett, Nairo Quintana

One long-established Spanish team and two British companies, Endura and Drag2Zero, joined forces to pool their expertise and produce a range of aerodynamic clothing for the team riders.

This aero jersey manages to combine a very reasonable consumer price with some nice features, including the raw-edge silicon grippers, an invisible YKK zip, and use of ColdBlack treatment to reflect the heat on this predominantly navy design.

2014
BELKIN/ LINKSYS/ BIANCHI/ SANTINI TEAM JERSEY

Manufacturer: Santini

Associated bike: Bianchi

Key riders: Lars Boom, Sep Vanmarcke

Etxeondo had created the 2013 version of this team's jersey (although the jerseys were branded as Giant), but in 2014 Santini announced they would support the team's clothing, shortly after Bianchi announced they would provide the team's bikes.

This aero jersey is very similar in construction to the Orica/ GreenEDGE jersey (see page 194) and uses a variety of fabrics to provide the best, aerodynamic fit for the pro riders.

2014
GIANT/SHIMANO TEAM JERSEY

Manufacturer: Etxeondo

Associated bike: Giant

Key rider: Marcel Kittel

This Giant/Shimano summer climber's jersey is made by Etxeondo from an extremely elastic and aerodynamic polyester material. It has some highly breathable open-mesh fabric panels, which help keep pro rider body temperatures down while they slip through the air.

To further aid the sprinters, Etxeondo developed a special all-in-one speed-suit. It had many of the aerodynamic advantages of a time trial speed-suit, but was designed for all-day comfort.

For the 2015 season, Etxeondo further experimented by using Dyneema fibres in the bib shorts to provide abrasion protection on the thighs when the riders crash.

2014
GB NATIONAL CHAMPION JERSEY WITH HARGROVES CYCLES/TRANT

Manufacturer: Capo

Associated bike: Specialized

Key rider: Ian Field

Hargroves Cycles is a long-established chain of bicycle shops in the south of England. Since 1981, the red and yellow kit of the Hargroves riders has been a common sight, particularly in the discipline of cyclo-cross.

Shop owner Peter Hargroves was a successful cyclo-cross rider himself, and is often seen in the pits helping riders with their bikes at top-level events.

This classic, elegant jersey is also signed by a number of the other team riders, many of whom are also National Champions in their own categories.

2015
GIANT/ALPECIN/ ETXEONDO TEAM JERSEY

Manufacturer: Etxeondo

Associated bike: Giant

Key riders: John Degenkolb, Tom Dumoulin

The Giant team management must have been delighted when John Degenkolb stepped up and took victories in Milan–San Remo and Paris–Roubaix in a stellar spring classics campaign.

Etxeondo, the team's technical clothing sponsor, must have been equally pleased by the fact that the last rider to win these two races in the same year was Sean Kelly in 1986. Sean's iconic yellow KAS jersey was also made by the Basque clothing manufacturer and features on page 54.

This bold, powerful and dramatic jersey is a chance for Etxeondo to get their name back to the top of the European professional peloton after making the previous year's jersey (see page 211) under a white label deal with Giant.

2015
LOTTO/JUMBO/ BRAND LOYALTY/ BIANCHI TEAM JERSEY

Manufacturer: Santini

Associated bike: Bianchi

Key riders: Robert Gesink, Wilco Kelderman

This LottoNL/Jumbo aero jersey is very similar in construction to the Belkin 2014 jersey (see page 210), employing a variety of fabrics to provide the best fit.

Santini have used a covered zip to allow the riders full ventilation without cutting through the sponsors' logos. Yellow features prominently on the jersey, so Santini had to produce a slightly different version for the Tour de France, to avoid confusion with the event leader's jersey.

2015
TEAM SKY
TEAM JERSEY

Manufacturer: Rapha
Associated bike: Pinarello
Key rider: Chris Froome

Team Sky has up to 30 riders and they are expected to race from January to October. In November and December, they work hard on their pre-season preparation training, so the team as a whole requires a huge amount and a huge variety of clothing.

When Rapha took over the Team Sky sponsorship from Adidas for the 2013 season, they invested considerable time and money to ensure the riders were satisfied. Every rider has over 300 different items to wear, including bespoke tailored kit as well as personalized name garments. 2016 will be Rapha's last year sponsoring Team Sky.

Chosen by the riders for its versatility and consistently excellent performance, this aero jersey is treated with ColdBlack dye which absorbs less of the sun's heat and makes the jersey as cool to wear as a light-coloured one.

2015
SAXO BANK
TEAM JERSEY

Manufacturer: Sportful
Associated bike: Specialized
Key riders: Alberto Contador,
Peter Sagan

This unique kit was introduced before the official team jersey design was released. Team riders including Alberto Contador, Peter Sagan, and even the often outrageous Russian team owner Oleg Tinkoff were pictured using the kit and it caused quite a stir on social media sites.

Inspired by Napoli FC, this pro race jersey features a number of different fabrics (some aero, some mesh) for the best fit and I think it was a shame it was only used for training. In the modern peloton, it's nice to see a light-hearted design that isn't all about corporate guidelines.

The team later introduced a new race kit with a more subtle camouflage design for the 2015 Tour de France. They used fluorescent yellow to ensure their riders were clearly distinguishable from the race leader.

2015
CANNONDALE/ GARMIN TEAM TOUR DE FRANCE JERSEY

Manufacturer: Castelli

Associated bike: Cannondale

Key riders: Dan Martin, Ryder Hesjedal

In 2015, the Cannondale/Garmin team released a new special edition kit which their riders wore for the three weeks of the Tour de France. It was a dramatic change: out went the almost subtle, predominantly black design and in came this lime-green affair, complete with touches of blue to hint at previous Garmin kits.

Castelli, who had previously developed new clothing designs with the Cervélo TestTeam in the Tour de France, designed this new kit to be comfortable and lightweight, and chose a lighter colour to help to reflect the heat.

2015
MTN/QHUBEKA TEAM JERSEY

Manufacturer: Castelli

Associated bike: Cervélo

Key riders: Daniel Teklehaimanot, Steve Cummings

Are the vertical stripes influenced by the Juventus football team, the GS Carpana cycle jersey from the sixties, or zebras from the African plains? This 2015 design was a departure from the predominately black, and some would argue more classy, kit the team wore in 2014.

There is no doubt this design is easy to spot in the peloton – although that didn't stop Steve Cummings slipping past the French duo of Thibaut Pinot and Romain Bardet on his way to a stage victory at the Tour de France. Daniel Teklehaimanot also had a successful Tour, taking the King of the Mountains jersey for four days, the first black African to wear it.

2015
TEAM WIGGINS TEAM JERSEY

Manufacturer: Rapha

Associated bike: Pinarello

Key rider: Bradley Wiggins

Team Wiggins has been built around Sir Bradley Wiggins, whose career highlights merit a book of their own. He's the winner of the 2012 Tour de France and the world hour record holder, and he has won seven Olympic Medals, including four golds.

This exact jersey is a team-issue garment, identical to those worn by Sir Bradley and his UCI Continental team mates, and not available from the Rapha online store. Its mid-weight fabric provides some protection from cold air and wicks away moisture, perfect for those typically British and Belgian early- and late-season events. The design is clearly influenced by the British national kit of the eighties, as well as Mod culture, which is represented by the numerous roundels on the jersey design.

INDEX

PICTURE CREDITS

THANKS

While it has my name on the front cover, this book would not have been possible without the support, assistance, and patience of a number of people. It has been a team effort.

I created a blog about my cycle jersey collection to make use of the many skills that I learned during my Computing studies at the Open University. So I credit the Open University with kickstarting this project.

I'd like to thank my wife Elley and kids Brandon and Isabelle for their patience while I was researching and writing the book. I spent many an evening and weekend working behind a laptop, so I hope they are proud of the end result.

My boss, Mick Tarrant of Prendas Ciclismo, also deserves a mention. There is nothing the two of us like more than looking through old copies of *Winning* magazine and talking about the time when we first started cycling. Working at Prendas is always varied and, although the warehouse can get a little cold in the winter, it's a happy place to work.

It was Joe Cottingham of Octopus Publishing Group who first contacted me out of the blue and suggested that I should turn the contents of my blog into a book. With the blog as a starting point, I went about creating more in-depth text to accompany each jersey photograph. This was then expertly edited by Joanna Smith. Leanne Bryan then took over the day-to-day management of the project, making sure that every aspect of the book was as good as it could possibly be.

Andy Storey

Commissioning Editor Joe Cottingham | **Creative Director** Jonathan Christie | **Senior Editor** Leanne Bryan | **Designer** www.theoakstudio.co.uk | **Photographer** Richard Clatworthy | **Copy Editor** Joanna Smith | **Picture Researcher** Jen Veall | **Production Controller** Sarah Kramer

An Hachette UK Company
www.hachette.co.uk

First published in Great Britain in 2016 by Mitchell Beazley, a division of Octopus Publishing Group Ltd, Carmelite House, 50 Victoria Embankment, London EC4Y 0DZ
www.octopusbooks.co.uk
www.octopusbooksusa.com

Design and layout copyright © Octopus Publishing Group Ltd 2016 | Text copyright © Andy Storey 2016

Distributed in the US by Hachette Book Group, 1290 Avenue of the Americas, 4th and 5th Floors, New York, NY 10020

Distributed in Canada by Canadian Manda Group, 664 Annette St, Toronto, Ontario, Canada M6S 2C8

ISBN 978-1-78472-166-4

A CIP catalogue record for this book is available from the British Library.

Printed and bound in China.

10 9 8 7 6 5 4 3 2 1